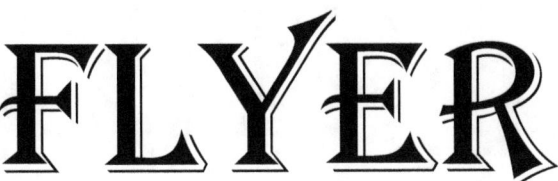

By
David Lee

Copyrights ©2025 by David Lee
All Rights Reserved.

This is a work of fiction. Whenever real persons, places, firms, institutions or events are mentioned, they are used fictionally, and any resemblance to actual persons, places, firms, institutions or events is coincidental.

Acknowledgements

*The author is grateful to **John Pissara, Roie Black,** and, in particular, **Art Wallhausen**, for advice and encouragement, and to **Ellen James** for valuable editing.*

The author also wishes to thank the following for their permissions and use of images:

- **Claudio Kirner (Pixabay)** for the picture on page 13.
- **Wright State University** for the licensed use of the picture of a Wright B Flyer and pilot on page 36.
- **The World War 1 Aviation Heritage Trust** for kindly authorizing the use of the picture of a Nieuport 17 on page 72.
- **Harald Landsrath** for the picture of George on page 76.

PART ONE

Chapter 1

THE CIRCUS WILL SHOW

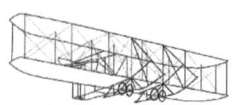

Midsummer twilight cast shadows on the strip of fescue and grama grass between the prop tent and the big top. Cramped inside the longest of five colorfully painted wagons parked in the strip, breathing air smelling of oil and gasoline and buzzing with the racket of two small gasoline engines, Frank Ellis yanked a cord to start a third motor. Crossing two fingers of his left hand, with his right, he levered the clutch that coupled the now-rattling engine to the big 40-horsepower motor-generator that filled most of the wagon.

Gears whined, and Frank held his breath until suddenly the big engine's thunder shook the wagon. Thankfully, raising cramped legs from plank flooring and collecting scattered tools, Frank smiled through the bars that made up the wagon's side and waved to the woman seated in a wheelchair outside.

"Well, Mother," he shouted, "The A&E will show tonight!" She arched her brows and looked hard at her son, her expression saying clearer than words, "For your sake, it had better!"

Pulling on the shirt he'd put aside to tackle the engine, Frank didn't notice female eyes watching his well-knit body at work through a small tear in the prop tent wall. His mother noticed.

Very little that happened in the Audrey - Ellis circus escaped Martha Ellis. She owned the show, left to her five years ago by her father, William "Bill" Eagan. There never was an Audrey – on setting out with the residue of two failed wagon circuses that he'd managed to buy and was struggling to will into unified life, Bill thought two names were better than one, and "Audrey" looked and sounded nice.

Martha had loved her father and wanted passionately to keep his circus alive for his memory. It was never an easy task, but she continued it devotedly.

Before leaving the wagon, Frank checked the meters on the power wagon's rear wall. Voltages correct; current from the generators driven by the small engines just about right for the incandescent lamps, which, in this year of 1911, lit dressing rooms, ticket office, and the big top's aisles.

He hopped lightly from the top step of the temporary stairs giving access to the power wagon. "Red wagon?" he asked. "Yes," answered the woman in the wheelchair, and he wheeled her to the A&E office wagon.

Frank Ellis made his way to the big top, with a detour to the cook tent, where a doughnut placated the adolescent hunger that hadn't quite left his twenty-year-old body.

Inside the big top, arc lights glared over the center ring and the broad sawdust-covered parade aisle that separated the ring from the seats now filling with two hundred people who had paid a half-dollar each (children under 10 accompanied by an adult entered free) to spend two and a half hours in a magical place.

Preparing to start the magic, bandmaster Paul Kieth took his silver cornet from beneath his left arm. Holding the instrument high in his right hand and lifting his left arm, he stood perfectly still for a moment. Then, as he brought both arms down for the downbeat, the fifteen-member A&E band crashed into the opening bars of "Entry of the Gladiators."

As if conjured out of the darkness of the covered walkway leading from the prop tent to the big top, clowns and acrobats spun onto the parade aisle in front of the audience. They danced and tumbled along, leading four handsomely tricked-out horses and riders. Behind them came two horses pacing side-by-side, bearing a slender rider standing with one foot on each horse. Smiling but aloof, she held her arms akimbo. Many in the audience realized the brilliance of this feat, and a wave of applause moved through the crowd, following her progress. That fall, she was eighteen years old.

Paul led the band into "Columbia, the Gem of the Ocean" to bring on A&E's prize possession, two African elephants. Their mahouts (natives, certainly, but of Purdy, Arkansas, not Kinshasa) had done their charges proud. Gleaming black and white designs covered the elephants' foreheads, red circles outlined their eyes, and the A & E logo blazed from red cloth shields on their foreheads.

Putting his cornet to his lips, Paul played a fanfare and cued the band into "Ride of the Valkyries" as an ornate cage wagon bearing a lion and lioness followed the elephants. Behind that menacing entry came more animals, but these, thoroughly domestic, were a tumble of small dogs in an open automobile, driven by their trainer, chubby Otto Karsch, who smiled his delight to be in such a magnificent show. Abandoning the Valkyries, Paul and the band had gone back to "Entry of the Gladiators" for the dogs.

Menace and "Ride of the Valkyries" returned as Otto's car drew away, with two tigers in a cage wagon. Tension increased yet more, as brilliant spotlights struck an almost new Ford Model T touring car, splendidly painted red with white trim, bearing two men and two women. Silver trapeze designs on the car's doors showed that there were the aerialists, who would fly high above the ring, risking death at each performance.

Attention fixed on the parade kept the audience unaware of the scene building in the ring, until the spotlights moved from the parade onto a pioneer family's prairie home, with mother and children on a porch, father coming home from the field. Paul artfully wove sections of "Home, Sweet Home" into the band's music.

Suddenly – as Paul's borrowed phrases switched to parts of Wagner's "Der Fliegende Hollander" – eight bareback riders with feathered head-dresses thundered onto the scene, circling the little homestead as mother hurried her tiny son and daughter indoors and father grabbed his rifle to defend his family. But alas, father is hit! He staggers against his door. Is all lost?

No! The band blares out the chorus of "Battle Hymn of the Republic," and four blue-coated riders sweep in to rout the redskins. Reviving, father staggers to his feet, held in mother's arms, as the little daughter rushes up to kiss the leader of the rescuers. Relieved, overjoyed, the crowd stood and clapped and whistled and whistled and clapped.

Vanishing from the tender scene, two spotlights revealed the ringmaster – who circus people called the "announcer" - standing in the center of the ring, striking in formal evening wear. "Ladies and Gentlemen," he said, speaking slowly in a wonderfully powerful voice, "Welcome to the Audrey and Ellis Circus, for an evening of magic and delight!"

The spotlights shifted to the front of the ring. The music shifted from triumphant to chill. A masked clown dressed in white ran into the light, accompanied by a small dog. Obviously terrified, the clown stopped, crouching with hands on knees, gasping for breath and looking anxiously back. Paul stopped the band.

In the silence, two massive figures loomed up in the darkness just beyond the lights. They marched inexorably into the ring as clown and dog scampered away to safety out of the ring, and the band swept into the triumphal march from "Aida."

"Ladies and Gentlemen," boomed the ringmaster, "Presenting Tusker and Shannah, Audrey and Ellis' magnificent African elephants!"

Parading around the ring accompanied by their mahouts, Tusker and Shannah were indeed magnificent. The A & E logo in ornate gold script blazed from scarlet cloth banners on their foreheads, and deep red blankets covered their broad backs.

Their mahout's severe black military uniforms thoroughly obscured Michael and George Watkinson of Rudy, Arkansas. Working in shows with large animals for nearly twenty years hadn't changed the brothers' northwest Arkansas characters, nor their speech. The mystery they projected was intact as they guided their charges through their act. The mahouts never spoke and never touched the elephants. The crowd saw them as figures of oriental mystery.

Mike and George walked beside their charges once around the ring as roustabouts rolled out three circular stands, two small and one much larger. Facing opposite directions to cover the whole row of seats, Tusker and Shannah each placed a huge foot on a small stand. At a gesture from the mahouts, the elephants rose on their hind feet and arched their trunks.

Both elephants stepped down from their stands. At a motion from his mahout, Tusker moved beside the large stand. The mahout gestured again, and Tusker placed his forefeet, and then, almost unbelievably for so large a creature, tucked his hind feet onto the stand. There he stood, enormous and yet somehow dainty, entrancing the crowd.

At an almost imperceptible signal from his mahout, Tusker got down from the stand. Suddenly, a girl in a spangled red costume ran up to Shannah, who bent her right leg to give the girl a perch. The girl jumped onto Shannah's curved leg, then lightly danced up to sit on the elephant's broad neck.

As Tusker bent his right leg, the white-clad clown ran back into the ring. Not at all afraid now, the clown swarmed up onto Tusker's leg and on up onto his neck, extending both arms.

The elephants paraded once more around the ring, their riders gaily waving to the crowd, and disappeared into the shadows from which they came.

At ringside, Frank Ellis and his father, the Ringmaster, watched the two broad backsides depart. "Hear 'em holler," said Frank.

"Yeah. Worth all they cost, and all we spend keepin' 'em," said the Ringmaster with a satisfied grin. Shifting into his powerful announcer's voice, he blared, "And now, ladies and gentlemen, boys and girls…

In the Red Wagon – the Audrey & Ellis Circus office – Fred and Martha Ellis reviewed the day's take with Dan Wilson, office manager.

"It's not good, Martha," Dan said. "1911 just isn't shaping up like last year. We'll be lucky to clear enough to pay off the bank when the season ends."

"Well, we can't quit until then," she replied. "Can we cut expenses anywhere?"

"I don't see how, without firing people or cutting back on what we feed 'em. And you never will do either of those."

"Got any ideas, Fred?"

"I don't. Frank has been sorta dreaming about adding a modern act. He talks about an aeroplane."

"An aeroplane! Sounds like pie in the sky. What would it cost us, I wonder?"

The Audrey–Ellis Circus top management was Martha Ellis, owner, Fred Ellis, her husband, and Frank Ellis, her son. Martha convened a meeting the next morning.

Chapter 2
A RISK WORTH TAKING

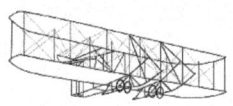

"Five thousand dollars!" Martha Ellis exclaimed, half rising from her chair. "That's twice as much as we clear in a whole season!"

"Yes, Mother," said Frank, "And the Wrights also make buyers pay $250 to train a pilot in their flying school."

"And just how could A&E get any good out of such an expense?" asked Martha.

"By selling more tickets and getting fees for the flying exhibits," answered Frank.

"We spend the whole season showing at county fairs and races, and sometimes standing alone, hoping to pull a crowd. The Wright Brothers are sending out trained flyers to show off their aeroplanes at fairs and races, some of them no larger than our stands, and they're getting big crowds.

"Newspapers give lots of space to flying. If A&E offered flying exhibitions, the extra publicity would guarantee us filling half again as many seats at every show. And here, I've worked it out. If we made just six flying exhibitions per season, and got a two-hundred-and-fifty-dollar fee for each, and if the publicity got A&L a thirty-three percent bump in ticket sales – and I admit we'd need to buy more seats – then we could pay off the cost of the plane and training in three seasons."

"That's three pretty big 'if's," said Fred Ellis. "And, we've got just thirty-five hundred in the bank. And, I don't see the Bank of Purdy loaning us anything like five thousand two hundred and fifty dollars in addition to the five hundred we borrow to get the season started."

"Yes," said Frank. "Actually, I'd been thinking about getting Aunt Mary to finance us."

"My sister is a smart old lady," said his mother. "You really think you could sell her this?"

"Well," Frank said, "Can I have a go?"

Martha was silent. Frank and his father waited.

She was used to using dangerous acts. Over the years, A&E had had a few bad injuries, and, though she never mentioned it, she couldn't forget that two performers had died in A&E's big top. The last time, the dying aerialist had fallen almost at her feet, his shocked eyes staring into hers as life faded from them.

Martha Ellis loved her son and secretly gloried in the daring that went with strength in the man she'd carried and brought into the world. Well, he was a man, and good men dared. "O.K., go see her. See what she says. Bring your figures. Your aunt is sharp with numbers."

It took three visits. Frank went away from the first certain he'd failed to persuade his aunt, though she had sent him away with specific questions to answer. There were more questions in the second meeting, but Mary asked them with interest and real understanding. And at the third meeting, she smiled and said, "O.k., bring me the Wright's contract. I'll let lawyer Madison see it, and you'll get the money, the whole five thousand two fifty – if he says it's all right. This will be a personal loan to you, Frank. Your folks will have enough to swing, expanding A&E's seats, and I don't want a lien on A&E's property. I want 3 per cent annual interest, payable at the end of each year's run, and I'll expect A & E to take out hull insurance on the machine if you can get it, and make sure the flying is covered by A & E's liability insurance."

Mary never told Frank that that day she made a codicil in her will forgiving the loan at her death.

Good grief, my nephew is handsome. Tom Madison advised against his project. It is a lot of money. Maybe I'm letting my heart rule my head with this, but Harry's money–oh, honey, how I miss you–lets me do things.

Like his mother, Frank Ellis took good care of A & E. He was going away to the Wright Aeronautical Academy, and Dan Jones, who managed A & E's electrical systems, was leaving the circus, so Frank needed someone to take over that key job. He motioned to roustabout Bob Petty, who joined him.

Together, the two men strode toward the noisy generator wagon. Stopping close enough to see through the wagon's bars but sufficiently far outside to hear over the generators' racket, Frank turned to face Bob and said, "Did you know that Dan Jones is leaving the show?"

"No. He has a pretty big job, doesn't he?"

"Yes. Dan takes care of all the A & E electric systems – dressing tents, ticket and office wagons, all the illumination lights in the Big

Top, and the spots to light the acts. He's got three guys working under him."

"Big job, all right. Why are you telling me about it?"

"Because I want you to start working with Dan tonight. You'll learn how to do all the jobs his crew handles. And I want you to learn how to do Dan's job. And as soon as Dan agrees that you can handle it, he'll leave, and you'll take over."

Bob stared, dumbfounded. "Why in God's name would you pick me? Why not one of Dan's guys?"

"Because I see you reading Scientific American when you get a break. Dan's guys just do the jobs Dan taught them. Not one of them thinks about the whole electric setup, and how it fits into the show, and how the equipment works. Do you want the job?"

"How does Dan feel about this?"

"He agrees. And he's in a hurry to leave. His dad died, leaving the family drugstore to Dan's brother, who wants Dan home pronto to be a partner." Do you want the job?

Bob said nothing, thinking hard. "Well," he said finally, and very firmly, "O. k."

Frank grinned. "Good. I'm surprised you didn't ask about pay. You'll get half of what Dan got, to start, and that'll go up by 50% when Dan leaves. You'll also get Dan's quarters when he goes. It's a good step up from what you're earning now."

Frank shook Bob's hand and said, "O. k. We might as well start now. The three generators in this wagon run incandescent lights all over the lot. The two little fellows take care of lighting outside the Big Top, and they run all the time. They keep the lights on in the dressing rooms, ticket wagon, and office wagon. They're the first electric lighting we had. Mother – Mrs. Ellis to you – needed a convincing demonstration before agreeing to electrify A & E. You see the two fuel tanks beside them? That arrangement lets those guys run steadily, without stops for refueling during preparation and show. Now come on into the juice wagon – yeah, I call it the same as everybody on the lot -- and we'll look into the meters and wiring."

Starting that day, Bob learned a lot about electricity, first at A & E, then more when he used his savings to study electrical engineering at the University of Arkansas in Fayetteville, when Ringling absorbed A & E in 1916. He ended his career as a vice president of the Westinghouse Corporation, living in Pittsburgh. But telling all that would take us too far away from our story.

PART TWO

Chapter 3
THE WRIGHT ACADEMY

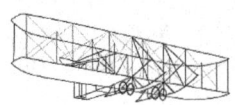

Frank Ellis, a dutiful son who genuinely loved his parents, wrote letters home while learning to fly at the Wright Aeronautical Academy. His high school English teacher had always complimented Frank's writing.

Sunday, May 7, 1912

Dear Mother and Father,

Thank you and Aunt Mary again for deciding that A&E should buy an aeroplane. And thank you all again for sending me to meet the Wrights' condition that a pilot they train must be available to fly their machine. You can depend on me to work hard to pass their course. I will also work hard to write to you and keep you up-to-date on progress. Remember that Mrs. Marshall said my essays in her English class surprised her!

It's quite a way from Purdy to Dayton. You saw me off at the A&E siding Saturday morning on the first bob-train to Fort Smith. Then I went on the Frisco from Ft Smith to Springfield and St. Louis. Changed to the Pennsy at St. Louis, for Indianapolis and then Dayton.

Passed through lots of towns A&E has played, Rogers and Springdale and Monett, Lebanon and Dixon and Mansfield (remember, Dad, how you swore at Dixon and said A&E would never play that – er, miserable place – again, and wished you had the money to buy it and burn it?)

The whole trip took a day and a night and a half. I got sandwiches on the train and got off for a real meal twice at long stops. Sleeping on the train was no problem for an old trouper, but sometimes I wished an A&E sleeper was handy! The trip was kind of like going on a real long hurry-up with A&E.

It seems strange not to be with A&E at the start of the season.

The train got to Dayton a little after noon on Friday. The railroad station at Dayton is really something! It has a tall tower that you can see all over town. Not too sure how that helps running trains, but it sure does take the eye.

Took a cab to 432 McCall Street, Mrs. Barnes' house. You can write to me at that address.

Mrs. Barnes is a widow. She rents three rooms, all of them now taken by men just about to start at the Wright Flying school. You may remember that Mr. Brookins recommended her in his letter welcoming me to the school.

Mrs. Barnes' place seems very respectable. Well, after all, the Wright brothers are a preacher's sons, so I'm sure any place their school recommends must be all right! Judging by her meals the last two days, Mrs. Barnes is a very good cook! Her daughter Pamela helps her keep house.

Mrs. Barnes' house is just a block away from the streetcar line that runs out to the Wright Flying school, in a field named "Huffman Prairie," for its owner, a banker, Mr. Torrance Huffman. The streetcar stop is Simms Station. Most of the training is there, but the course begins at the Wright Aeroplane Company factory, downtown in Dayton. It's an easy walk from Mrs. Barnes'. I'll be there by 8 tomorrow morning, before work starts at the factory.

**Love,
Frank**

Oh, he's a fine one, this Frank Ellis! Knocks politely at the door – you can tell a lot about a man by the way he knocks on a door. Some just bang away like they own the place. That kind always gives trouble.

He's big and good-looking, too. I'll have to watch out for Pammy with this one. And you watch yourself, Kathleen Barnes. Doesn't do to get fond of a lodger!

Well, now we're full up. Gonna keep ma and me busy. They all seem o.k., they're clean, and they're respectful to me, and they don't flirt with me – well, maybe a little. Of course, a girl likes a little of that, so long as it doesn't go too far! Bill is skinny, and Dave is a little fat. Frank's polite, and he seems to have been around the block some. I like his hair. Watch yourself, Pammy Barnes!

Monday, May 8, 1912

Dear Mother and Father,

Walked to the Wright factory with the two other new students who live at Mrs. Barnes', Bill Jones and Dave Galet. We're all about the same age. We got to the plant a little before eight, and the day's work was just starting.

Mr. Walter Brookins met us. He is an experienced flyer, but he doesn't seem much older than Dave and Bill and me. I gave him the A&E check for $250 to pay for the training. Mother left the date blank, and I dated it May 8, 1912, so Dan can enter that in the book.

Bill and Dave ponied up their fees – Bill handed over cold cash! – and Mr. Brookins (he says to call him Walt, and I'm trying to remember that) began our training right away. He started off by explaining how the course is organized.

We'd start in the plant, he said, to learn about how the aeroplanes are built. Understanding that would give us confidence in the planes and teach us to respect them. That's what Walt said – "respect" the planes. Funny, that's how I always feel about machines, like A&E's electric dynamos, when I've learned how they're put together and how they work.

After learning about how the planes are made, we'll begin learning to fly them by working on one fixed inside the plant. It doesn't fly, but with it we'll get used to the controls, how they feel and how they move. When Walt feels we're ready, the course will move to the Huffman prairie. Then we'll begin actually flying. The course lasts just ten flying days, so we need to get on the way!

After Walt's talk, we went into the plant. Walt explained what goes on in the separate rooms. The planes' parts are built separately, and then put together in the area of the plant Walt called "assembly."

The aeroplane is a lot more complicated than I expected. Take the wings, for instance. They're complicated, all right. To see how they're made, take an open Venetian blind. Replace the strings with wood shafts to make the thing hold its shape. Then go along the blind from top to bottom, and cut each slat into the shape that you want the wing to have at that particular distance from its end. Round each slat off on its left end, and taper its right end to about an eighth of its original width. Now cut four or five oval holes in each slat, and make the holes smaller as the slat tapers from the left end to the right one. Make a thin cloth sack to cover the whole thing, pull it over the blind from top to bottom, snug it up tight, and there's your wing! The holes make the wings light, while keeping them strong. Walt says the wings' exact shapes have a lot to do with the way the plane flies. The "sacks" that cover the wings are muslin cloth.

A lot of women work in the plant! They put the wing-shaped strips together, sitting side-by-side at tables.

Women stitch the muslin onto the frames. The stitching has to be perfect, or the wind flowing over the machine would pull the fabric off and crash the plane. While Walt explained this, Dan and Bill looked thoughtfully at the women sewing up aeroplanes, and I suppose I did, too. Talk about your life hanging by a thread!

We're due back at the factory tomorrow.

Love,
Frank

These guys seem ok, no trouble about money - all paid up. All three seem fit enough. Bill's on the skinny side, but not enough to worry about. Frank's older than me, and he acts like he's used to running things. Fine, so long as he pays attention and doesn't think he can pilot a plane until he can. Dave doesn't say much. No problem there, so long as he isn't slow. Gotta be quick to keep up with a plane. All three seemed to listen while I yakked away as we walked through the plant. Bill and Frank asked questions; Frank's were pretty smart, and Bill's were kinda dumb. Dave worries me a little. He didn't say anything. Well, that's a lot better than know-it-all!

Thursday, May 11, 1912

Dear Son,

Your mother and I were glad to have your letter of May 8. We got it yesterday. Pretty good mail service, Dayton to Purdy in just two days!

Mrs. Barnes' place sounds okay. k., and I'm glad to hear she sets a good table. We're glad you'll have company where you're staying.

It's good that the Wright school takes things slow and steady. Just one thing, Son, don't say things like "life hanging by a thread" when you write. Your mother worries.

Your father,
Fred Ellis

Chapter 4

CAREFUL FIRST STEPS

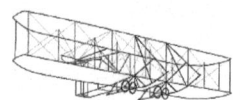

May 13, 1912

Dear Mother and Father,

Well, the last three days have been right busy. Every day, Walt Brookins kept Bill and Dave and me hard at it from 8 am until six, and I think he stopped then only because the plant closed up and the lights went off and the night watchmen came in.

Tuesday and Wednesday, and Thursday, we worked through each department in the plant. First was the blueprint office with complete blueprints for every part of the Wright B flyer. That's important for us, because as pilots we'll be expected to guide mechanics to the right blueprints for any damaged part. The Wright Company will send a mechanic to any operator of a Wright B that needs help, but it saves a lot of time if the pilot can give a local mechanic the information needed to make repairs, and, if necessary, to order replacement parts from the Company.

I'm no stranger to blueprints and diagrams, but I found this part of the course really tough. Poor Bill struggled, and Walt had to spend a lot of time with him.

But Dave was a real surprise. He is obviously right at home in blueprints, and his questions sometimes made Walt stop and think. And Dave's the guy who hardly ever says one word! Talk about still waters running deep.

After the blueprint office, it was interesting to see women putting small parts together and to see them stitch the skins onto wings.

Watching carpenters make the wood pieces for the Flyer's structure was an education in their craft. They check each piece to make sure that it matches its blueprint. You might think that the carpenters would get to know the parts' shapes without checking with the blueprints, but they always do check, three times. There's the old carpenter's saying, "measure twice, cut once," but Wright's carpenters go that one better. Walt says that's the way the Wright brothers do everything – they leave nothing to chance. Each piece is sanded and varnished three times, too.

Woodworkers make the propellers' complicated shapes. Walt says a propeller is sort of like a wing, but instead of using air flow to make the lifting force that holds the aeroplane up, the propeller pushes the air along to force the plane through the air. He says a propeller is a lot more complicated than a wing, because, since the propeller is spinning, each part of the propeller moves faster through the air the farther it is from the hub.

Walt made us really dig in on the blueprints, and he did even more with the engines. A pilot has to know the engine well enough to be able to make absolutely sure it is ready to fly before taking off.

The Wright's engines are really special. They are developments from the one in the Wright Flyer that made the first successful aeroplane flight, back in 1903. They deliver 35 hp, only a bit less than the big engine for A&E's main lighting plant, and they weigh only a little more than half as much. They're miracles!

Our last stop in the plant was the assembly area. It takes up all of one of the plant's two buildings. There, finally, you see the aeroplane take shape. Like every job in the Wright Company plant, assembly is done slow and steady, with many checks. Walt says it is very important that every aeroplane conforms exactly to the design. Even a fraction of an inch off can make the machine fly poorly, or dangerously, or even not at all!

We got through with the assembly area just at quitting time on Thursday afternoon. Walt said he was sure all three of us were ready to move on to the next step. Friday, we start working with a special training machine in the plant.

Love,

Frank

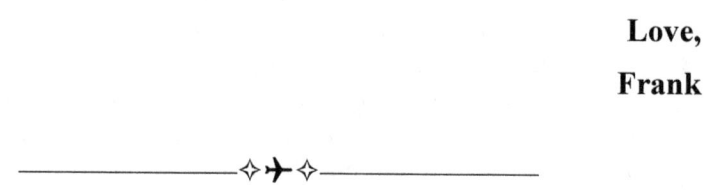

It was a pleasant, warm spring evening in Dayton. Pam Barnes stood outside the Barnes' front door, enjoying it, as Frank Ellis stepped out for a breath of air.

"Hi, Frank," Pam said. "How are you tonight?"

He was lonely. On the spur of the moment, he said, "Well, there's a movie just down McCall. You want to go see what's showing?"

Pam knew her mother wouldn't like this. "Sure," she said.

Chapter 5

ALOFT AT LAST

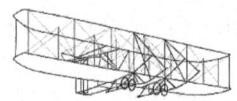

Sunday, May 14, 1912

Dear Mother and Father,

Well, we may not be pilots just yet, but Bill and Dave and I sure have spent a lot of time in the Wright B Flyer! Friday, we came to the plant, downtown in Dayton, just like on Monday through Thursday, and went right away to the big room at the back of the assembly building.

What looks like a Flyer is sitting there, but it's really a rig for training. It doesn't fly. Students get into it just as they would with a real machine. It has controls just like the real plane's, so students can get used to how they feel and move.

The Flyer is big. When you come up close, like you were going to get in it, the wings seem to stretch out forever on both sides. I said "get in," but it's really more like you get on it. You sit on the front edge of the bottom wing. Your feet go out to a bar for support, and your hands hold two rods for controlling the machine. There's a chair-back to help you sit upright.

The rod in your left hand lets you bring the nose of the plane up or down, and the one in your right hand lets you twist the wings and turn the rudder together, to make turns. Walt explained that the machines we'll actually fly will have an additional lever on top of the right-hand rod to move the rudder independently.

Walt says that the pilot and the engine sit well forward, because the wing's lifting force is concentrated near the front of the wings. And the passenger seat is to the right of the pilot's, closer to the engine. The pilot sits a bit to the left of the Flyer's center. That's because, Walt says, the lifting force is at the middle of the plane, so the machine's balance is nearly the same when the pilot is alone as when there's a passenger. Walt says that the pilot's main job is to keep the plane balanced all the time. He made me think flying the aeroplane would be like being on a sway pole![1]

The training machine has two sets of controls. That lets the "passenger" control it while instructing the student pilot.

Using a step-stool, Walt got into the instructor's seat and told Bill to climb in and go first. Bill used a stool and grabbed a strut with his left hand to swing himself on board.

Walt said, "O. k.," and three mechanics pulled supports out from under the trainer, one from each side of the bottom wing and one from under the rudder. The trainer tipped slightly to the right, and the nose came up a bit.

"Well, let's fix that," said Walt. He used the lever in his right hand to pick up the right wing and moved his left hand to bring the nose down. Walt spoke to Bill. "Now, I'm going to tip the nose down, and then pull it back level. You take both controls, but don't move them, just follow their movements as I do it."

Walt did so and turned to Bill. "Ok, Bill, now I'm going to put the nose down again, and this time you bring it back."

The nose went down. Walt looked at Bill. "Ok, Bill, you've got it." Bill squared his shoulders, and the trainer's nose shot up. "Go easy," said Walt, "I've got it," and the nose came down to level. "Let's try again."

---

[1] A "sway pole" or "tippy pole" is about fifteen feet long, with a chair on one end. A rider held aloft in the chair swings through broad arcs while being carried along.

On the third try, Bill got the nose pretty well level, with just a couple of corrections at the end. Walt and Bob kept at it, going through rocking the wings to left and right, very slightly at first and then more and more.

Electric motors in the trainer machine warp the wings in response to the control inputs. This way, the student can see the wings' movements. The movements are quite small.

"Those last ones were more like what you'll do to make turns," Walt said. "Remember, when you turn the real plane, you need to lift the nose some or else you'll lose height. Now let's grab some lunch." Bill's armpits were dark with sweat.

After lunch, it was my turn. Walt took me through the same routine, and before he got through, I was sweating like Bill. Walt didn't say much. Toward the end of the exercise, controlling the training machine began to seem kind of natural.

Dave came last, and the quiet guy who never says much got along much better than either Bill or me. The three of us walked back to Mrs. Barnes' house, ready to wash up and change shirts, and get supper.

Thursday, we went through the same exercises at the plant. "Exercise" is the right word. It's not really hard to move the trainer's controls, but you have to think about what you're doing all the time. Today, mechanics standing beside the wings and tail pushed the trainer to wobble it as the three of us sweated. Walt said this was to give us the feel of the aeroplane in flight. "The air is bumpy," he said, "and the machine will tip over sideways or nose up or down if you let it. You have to fly it all the time."

When we left the plant Thursday evening, Walt said we'd graduated from this part of our training, and he'd meet us at

Huffman Prairie tomorrow morning at 8 to go on with actual aeroplanes.

Friday morning, Bill and Dave, and I got on the interurban at 7 am. It's about a half-hour ride out to the Simms Station. It's just a short walk from the Simms Station to the flying field, and we got there in good time to meet Walt at the hangars at 8 am. He said the weather was good for flying, and the four of us walked across the field to the north-east corner, where a Wright flyer was parked, facing into the light west wind. Two Wright mechanics stood beside the plane. Walt said hello and introduced Bill and Dave, and me to them. Their names are Ed Smith and Keith Wilson.

Walking up to the Flyer, I felt like I was meeting a person! The front and the wings of the real flyer are just the same as the trainer's, but the real machine stretches out both front and back, so it's almost as long as it is wide.

Walt told us students that we'd spend some time on two underpowered flyers, learning how to maneuver a flyer on the ground (Wright method again – take slow steps, and be careful!). But he told us that we'd begin today with short orientation flights.

Walt got on first, closest to the engine, and motioned me to get on. I got to go first!

The Flyer smells of gasoline and oil. The bottom wing has oil stains around the base of the engine, and the cloth of the wings and rudder and rear wing looks weathered. Well, those planes do a lot of work!

The controls on this plane had something added, compared to the trainer: the right-hand rod twists the wings, as in the trainer, but in the Flyer, a handle on top of that lever moves the rudder. In the trainer, the rudder was coupled to the wing-warping control and automatically moved just the amount needed for a turn.

At a nod from Walt, Ed and Kieth pulled on the propellers. They moved down, seemed to hesitate, and then started to spin as the engine caught.

The Wright engine makes a lot of noise. It shakes the plane. Sitting near it, on the bottom wing, you can feel the vibrations in your fanny. Walt reached out and put his hands on the two control rods.

Right away, we started rolling down the field. It was a bumpy ride – the Flyer doesn't have springs!

Presently, we were going like a flat-out Model T. Walt pulled back just a little with his left arm, the flyer bounced a couple of times, and the bumps stopped – we were flying!

The pasture seemed to drop away beneath us. I felt happy and proud and maybe just a little bit scared. Pretty soon, I was going to have to do this all by myself! Don't tell Jill I was scared.

Sure enough, the air is bumpy. Not sharp bumps like a car or a wagon, more like something was pushing and tugging the flyer as it went along. As we flew (flew!) along the flyer's nose would sort of wander slowly up and down. Walt's small, gentle motions with his left arm kept her under control.

The flying field at Huffman Prairie is a bit less than a mile long. Walt would fly for about a minute parallel to the interurban, then turn around and fly back for about a minute, keeping over the field. As he made the turns, he moved the handle on top of the right-hand rod to coordinate the rudder's movement with the twisting of the wings, and used his left arm to lift the nose up just a bit. Flying an aeroplane is a complicated business!

Walt had me put my hands on the dual controls, just the way we did in the trainer, and follow him through as he went above the north side of the field, turned, flew back above the south side, then went around again. As we started the second trip up the south side, Walt gave me a good, long look. "Think you can keep her straight and level for a while? Today I'll make the turns; you just handle the straights. You'll start with turns after you get comfortable with movements on the ground."

Of course, I said yes! I grasped the two control rods. Walt took his hands off, but kept them close. "O.k., you've got it," he said. I gulped.

I could feel the air-bumps in the controls! I managed to remember to make small, gentle movements of the controls as we flew over the long side of the field. I left the rudder lever alone.

The Wright B Flyer really keeps the pilot busy. She always wants to nose down, or nose up, or tip to the right, or tip to the left. Flying her really is kind of like being on a sway pole. You've got to be right with her every second. I was too busy to be scared.

I was really surprised to see how well the feel of the Flyer's controls matched the trainer's, and while I sure wasn't nearly as smooth as Walt, I did manage to keep us pretty nearly level, but I let the Flyer gain height all the time.

Walt took over the controls. "I've got it," he said. He smiled. "Pretty good," he said. We had come pretty far from the field's East boundary. Walt turned the flyer back West and lined us up with the path on which we'd taken off. He let the nose down, not much at all, and we began to lose height. Walt sort of aimed us at the start of the takeoff path.

He kept us going steadily down. As we crossed into the air over the field, he lifted the nose a bit, and we rounded out until we were flying level just above the grass.

Walt pulled a string attached to the engine to cut off fuel. The engine stopped. Walt just barely lifted the nose as the Flyer settled onto the grass. We stopped.

"Well," said Walt, "How did you like that, Mr. Ellis?"

I'd been tired and a little shaky after the trainer exercises, but they did me so much good that I just felt really happy after my first time at the Flyer's controls. The Wrights really know how to train pilots, just like they really know how to build aeroplanes. They are very careful about everything they do with aeroplanes.

Dave went next, then Bill. Friday, we practiced maneuvering a low-powered flyer on the ground, and Saturday, we graduated to training with a full-powered machine, making flights of 10 or 12 minutes. Walt kept us hard at it. The hardest thing I've done so far is making turns. Walt has us making turns to the left and to the right as we fly above the field.

We also fly "figure eights," first making a complete circle, turning to the left, then turning to the right for another full circle. I think I'm getting pretty good at controlling the Flyer, and watching from the ground as Bill or Dave practices makes me think they are, too, but Walt hasn't let any of us land her yet. I've now got just over an hour of time in control of the Flyer!

Love,

Frank

"Don't tell Jill I was scared," huh. Doesn't he realize she reads his letters just as eagerly as Fred and I do? She practically tears them out of our hands! I'd like to see anybody stop her. And why on earth don't they write to each other?

He sounds so happy. I doubt he was really scared in that aeroplane. He's just too stupid to get scared of anything. Thinks he's invincible. He is strong. He never says he misses me or his folks. He said he missed starting the season with A & E! Why doesn't he write to me? Has he got a girl in Dayton? What about that Pamela Barnes?

Chapter 6

A LICENSED PILOT

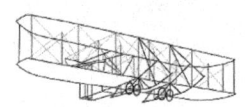

May 21, 1912

Dear Mother and Father,

Yesterday, May 20, 1912, I took the Flyer up all by myself, flew her around the field a couple of times, brought her down and landed. As Walt says, I "soloed." Silent Dave beat me to it - he went Friday afternoon – and Bill's big day will be tomorrow, I suppose.

Soloing ends the beginner's part of the course at the Wright Flying School. For the next two weeks, we'll work on the demonstrations we'll give. One of these is to fly in front of a crowd, turn, fly off about a hundred yards, then turn around and fly directly at them, pulling up just in time to fly safely over them. Another is the good old "figure eights." We do them in the course. There's also one in which we dive straight down, about 20 yards in front of the crowd, then level off about 30 feet from them and about 10 feet above the ground. Walt says he thinks the Wrights are going to stop this in their exhibitions, because it makes women faint in the crowd. It's safe enough, and I'm perfectly willing to do it for A&E, but honestly, I don't like the idea of scaring folks. Sure, the aerialist scare the crowd, but I'd rather A & E's flying made 'em delighted to see what the Wright Flyer can do, rather than scared.

Walt says the factory will start building A&E's aeroplane next week. She should be ready to go just about when my course ends. I hope so. Then we can meet in Purdy and get to work making money for A & E.

Walt says the Wright brothers encourage graduates of their School to get the Pilot's License of the International Aviation Federation, the Fédération Aéronautique Internationale. The Aero Club of America administers the award of licenses. They are very fussy, according to Walt. Anyway, Walt says the school will help students get their license.

I'm not sure it'd be worth A&E's money for their pilot to be licensed. Eventually, I suppose, the government will require licenses, so maybe it'd be good to have that done. Maybe I could be prepared for the license test by the end of the Wright Flying School program. What do you think?

Love,

Frank

Well, we did it, me and the flyer. It sure felt lonesome, alone in her left seat. Guess I never realized how much I relied on Walt until he wasn't there. The flyer picked up speed quicker with only one man aboard. She let me know she was ready to take off, just the way she always does, by the way the elevator control stiffened in my left hand, and the way she held off the ground a little more after each bounce. When she felt just right, I eased back just a little with my left arm, and she fairly jumped into the air. Honestly, I love this machine! I held her steady, just a little nose high, and she climbed up to about fifty feet, where we usually fly over the prairie. We just got to that height when it was time to turn so as to keep us over the school's field. By now, working all three controls together to make a turn seems natural. Press gently left or right with your right arm to warp the wing, pull with your left arm to bring the nose up just a bit, bring in some rudder with the right wrist, then hold all steady while she swings around almost to the new direction that you want.

Then gently undo all that, until she's steady and level on her new course. But you can't just sit in a flyer and expect her to stay straight and level. You have to fly her all the time, or she'll nose down, or nose up, or turn one way or another. Flying the Wright B Flyer really is kinda like riding a tippy pole. Walt told me to make two circuits, so of course I did. As we rounded out after the last turn on each circuit, I picked out the spot where I wanted to land and put her nose down, just a little. She responds a lot more with just one man aboard. I used all the controls now, elevator with the left arm, wing warping with the right arm and rudder with the right hand, playing all together, just little movements, more like just pressures, to keep us lined up on the spot as we flew down. As we got closer to the ground, the grass in the landing spot seemed to stay still, with the grass ahead of where we'd touch down moving away, and the grass behind where we'd touch down moving backward, faster and faster as we neared the grass. I pulled on the left rod to round us out just about right, with the wheels only about a foot above the grass. I held us just a moment to check our height. It looked pretty good, and I pulled the string to kill the motor. She slowed down, and as she did, I kept the elevator rod moving slowly back, lifting her nose little by little so she didn't lose height. When the speed got too slow to keep her flying, she dropped gently onto the grass. The first time, I had her a bit too high, but it was a pretty good landing. It's easy to either pull the nose up too fast, so she climbs and stalls out too high, or to pull up too slowly, so she smacks into the ground and bounces. Either mistake is hard on the flyer, and hard on the pilot, too, because everybody is watching the landing and you hate to look bad.

May 24, 1912

Dear Frank,

Get the license. The government will surely require that, eventually, and your mother and Aunt Mary and I all think it will be good business for A&E's pilot to have that certificate, particularly since we may wish to give aeroplane rides to favored customers.

Regarding customers, do you think A&E might be able to have aeroplane flights by July 4?

Your mother sends her love.

Your father,

Fred Ellis

May 27, 1912

Dear Father,

I'll try for the FAI license. Walt says there'll be no additional charge from the school, since the price of the aeroplane includes 1 hour of familiarization flight with a Wright instructor. Also, Bob Shaw, who has the FAI license and is, like Walt, an instructor in the Wright Academy, is willing to be my examiner. For his fee, he wants a bottle of champagne. That seems quite reasonable! Bob has scheduled the final part of the exam for Thursday, June 8.

Love to you and Mother,

Frank

June 3, 1912

Dear Mother and Father,

Today I passed out of the Wright Flying Academy course for pilots of Wright aeroplanes. Walt shook my hand and said I was a good pilot, and wished me luck on the FAI exam next Thursday.

I surely do want to pass that exam. I'm shamelessly begging extra time in the Academy's aeroplanes. I believe I can answer the questions about aeroplanes and flying, but it's easy to slip up on the actual flying. Aeroplanes are "nervous cattle!" Walt and the other instructors kindly look the other way when I get into an aeroplane for an extra flight, usually first thing in the morning, or last thing in the afternoon. I think the instructors, particularly Walt, really want me to get the FA license!

It's going to be lonesome at Ma Barnes' place. Bill and Dave have gone away, so for a few days I'll be her only boarder.

It's very good that you managed to play Fort Smith on June 10 and 11, with a break day on Sunday, June 12.

The Wright Company will send a mechanic with our Flyer to help us get her set up. I've asked them to send Ed Smith. I've worked with him all through the flying part of the course, and I'm sure people at A&E will find him easy to work with.

That brings me to a request. Could Bob Petty be assigned to work with me and Ed on the flyer? I could just manage to do the flying and maintenance, and transportation, but it sure would be better to have another head and pair of hands on the jobs. Bob could work with Ed and me as the flyer gets to work smoothly with A&E.

You asked if we could use the Flyer on July 4. I'm confident that we can. Let's plan for our Flyer to give exhibition flights, starting on the break day, Monday, June 12. Perhaps we could give some Fort Smith dignitaries rides as early as that day, to generate some newspaper publicity. The Tuesday that week is on the 13th, so maybe we should skip that date in case the clients are superstitious!

Love,

Frank

Western Union Telegram

Dayton, Ohio, 6 PM June 9, 1912

To: Mr. & Mrs. William Ellis, Ellis Ranch,

Rte 2, Purdy, Arkansas

From: Frank Ellis, Western Union Office, Dayton, Ohio

PASSED HOME SUNDAY, TELL JILL

Frank got to bed a little later than usual that night, his last in Mrs. Barnes' house. Still unwinding from the SAI license exam, and slightly tipsy from the celebratory dinner to which Walt Brookins and Bob Shaw had treated him, he was just drifting into sleep when light from the hall outlined widening and shrinking strips at the edge and top of the door to his room. Pam Barnes tiptoed across the carpet and slipped into bed beside him.

Gently, she caressed Frank's face and lay quietly close to him. "Hello," she said. "Are you a little lonesome tonight?"

Chapter 7

THE FLYER JOINS THE CIRCUS

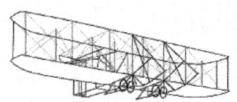

Mr. and Mrs. Fred Ellis, Frank Ellis, Jill Coffee, Bob Petty, and Ed Smith stood beside Martha's wheelchair, next to a sparkling new Wright B Flyer, parked on a well-mown twelve-acre pasture, close to the Ellis ranch house.

"Mother," said Frank, "I'll say it again: we all think you should be the first A & E passenger. Please let me help you onto the plane. Ed and I had her up this morning, and everything checks out fine."

"And, please excuse me for buttin' in," said Ed, "but I've seen lots of pilots' work, and, honestly, Frank's just about as good as they come, right up there with Mr. Brookins. I'll be honest, nobody's as smooth as Mr. Orville, but Frank's real good. Hardly anybody gets that good as fast as he did."

"I'm glad Frank's a good pilot," said Martha Ellis, "But I told you, I'm too old for adventure. Jill is A&E's star equestrienne, the show's star female artist. She should be first."

"We might as well give up," said Fred. "Martha has spoken."

"Well," said Frank, "I know when I'm licked. Please come over here, Jill, and I'll help you on board."

Thus, Miss Jill Coffee became the first passenger on the Audrey and Ellis Wright B Flyer, piloted by Frank Ellis. She had come togged out for riding, which worked out fine to control the breeze pouring over the flyer's passenger seat. When, later, a President's lady was given a flight, she tied a cord around her ankles to keep her long skirt modestly in place, and started the "hobble skirt" fad.

Well, there they go, flying away into the air. They certainly make a handsome couple. They seem friendly enough, and Jill couldn't wait to read Frank's letters when he was in Dayton learning to fly. Frank ought to marry, and so should she. What's holding them back?

Air sure is bumpy today. Generally, is, around noon on a sunny day. Gotta keep the flyer in line. Time to turn around and fly back. Nice turn, Frank! This flyer is a dandy. Women sure are stubborn cattle. Why did Mother push Jill into this? And why does Jill shy away whenever I try to get close to her? She's known me all her life. Am I ugly, or something? Oops – hellfire and damnation, I damn near let the flyer stick her nose up and stall. That's what I get for thinking about a woman, and not her!

Oh, gosh, Frank's gotta watch his business better! He damn near let the flyer pitch up and stall! What's the matter with him? He's a lot better pilot than that!

Goodness, this airplane bucks like a bronc! Oh! She really reared up then! Phew – Frank's got her in hand. Thought she was going to buck us off, there. Frank wants me to be his girl. I'd like that, too, but I'm a damn good rider, and I know I can get better. I'm not ready to give it up and settle down to keeping house and raising babies. And that's the wife he'd want, just like all men. Well, that's natural enough. I'd like to have his babies! Goodness, Jill Coffee, stop thinking about that! You can't do two tough full-time jobs at once, that's a fact, and keeping me and the horses fit for fancy riding is a tough full-time job! Oops – we're headin' down! Oh, I see, Frank's gonna land us. Golly, we're almost in the grass! Well, that was a bump – oh, we're landed! I've had an airplane ride!

Chapter 8
PUBLIC RELATIONS

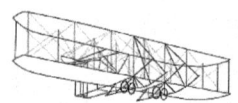

"What have you got us into, Frank? That man weighs three hundred pounds, if he weighs an ounce! That's too much for the flyer! You just might get her to climb, but then you'd break a spar the first gust you hit!" The idea of abusing a flyer really upset Ed Smith.

"Lordy, here he comes, with his wife. She sure is a pretty little thing! And Jill is comin' with 'em. And there's a guy with a camera!"

"Hello, Frank," said the striking beauty on Mayor Marshall's arm. "Haven't seen you in ages!"

"Hi, Mrs. Marshall," said Frank. He didn't remember his high school English teacher looking like that!

"Glen's just insisting that he won't go up in the airplane," she said. "We've been arguing that all the way out from Fort Smith."

"Well," said the mayor, "That Record photographer over here sure would rather have your picture for the paper than mine, Helen." Glen Marshall knew how to get people thinking well of him, and a pretty wife doing something interesting, like riding in an airplane, would do that quite nicely.

Thanks to a phone call from Jill, Helen had come in riding togs. She and Jill exchanged a knowing glance as Frank helped Helen aboard the airplane.

Northwest Arkansas Record, June 12, 1912

Northwest Arkansas's circus gem, the Audley and Ellis show, has joined the select group of modern shows to acquire an aeroplane. Their Wright machine has arrived at the A&E quarters in Purdy, and the show is introducing the air age by giving rides to local dignitaries. Fort Smith Mayor Glen Marshall was to be among that select group, but he deferred to his wife, Mrs. Helen Marshall. The top picture shows Mrs. Marshall being helped onto the A & E aeroplane by pilot Frank Ellis, and the bottom illustration shows the A & E aeroplane with Mrs. Marshall and Mr. Ellis in flight over Purdy.

Chapter 9

SHOWING WITH THE CIRCUS

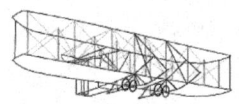

A&E first showed with their airplane at the Arkansas State Capitol, Little Rock, on Saturday, June 15, 1912, at the racetrack of the Pulaski County fairgrounds. The Arkansas Gazette had given the event plenty of publicity, and the Fairgrounds' grandstand and the overflow bleachers on both its sides were filled to capacity, maybe perhaps just a bit more.

Ed Smith, the Wright mechanic, and his apprentice, A&E's Bob Petty, had scrupulously cleaned and oiled and tightened to specification every part and every inch of the Flyer, twice, and then, in the best Wright tradition, gone over everything again.

Perfectly at home performing outside the big top, the A&E show began as usual. After the opening parade, the pioneer family appeared in the racetrack's infield. But when the Indians attacked, the blue-coated soldiers did not appear.

Bandleader Paul Kieth stopped the music. In the silence, the flyer's noisy approach turned heads to the left, and here she came, around the overflow bleachers, flying in front of the grandstand about level with the middle row of seats.

Climbing over the infield scene, Frank dived toward the attackers, flew low over them, and pulled up into a steep climbing turn that brought him back over the Indians. Again and again, he pulled up and turned back over the enemy. He kept this up in a figure-eight pattern as his foes broke away, fleeing for their lives as the soldiers appeared and chased them away.

Flying fifty yards away in front of the grandstand, Frank turned and flew straight toward the crowd. Closer he came, and as people in the grandstand began to edge uneasily away, he pulled up sharply to fly over the grandstand. Well clear of the crowd, Frank turned back to fly past the grandstand, dipping the flyer's wings alternately left and right, waving goodbye as he brought her out of the show.

The crowd had literally never seen anything like that. It was more than they could take in. They paid an audience's great tribute to the act, sitting in silence for a moment before standing as one person, and applauding, shouting, and applauding!

It was Jill Coffee's idea to incorporate the flyer into the opening spectacle. She wanted to give her horses a share in the airplane's glamor!

Oh, man, that was really something! I'm gonna write to Mr. Orville about that! He ought to know how Frank – and Jill – are really using their airplane!

The Ellis family council, Fred, Martha and Frank, with the Audrey-Ellis star rider Jill Coffee, was in session on Wednesday afternoon, June 19, 1912. Frank had the floor.

"We're going to show in Springfield, Missouri, for three days next month – the second, third and fourth. It's going to be a big time for Greene County; they're restarting the county fair for the first time in years. There'll be a big stock sale at the fairgrounds on the second and third, with fancy catalogs printed in Aurora. It's twenty-five miles on the road from Aurora to the Fair site. In the air, the distance is just twenty miles. The flyer makes a bit more than 40 miles per hour, so an Aurora – to – Springfield trip would take half an hour. Summer winds are usually around 12 miles an hour from the south-west, right along the direct route from Aurora to the fairground. Even half that wind speed would knock the time down to 26 minutes, and the full 12 would make it 23 minutes. Wright Flyers have made longer flights than that.

"A&E would get lots of publicity if we delivered the catalogs from Aurora by airplane. I've exchanged telegrams with Walt Brookins. He says the A&E flyer can do the trip.

"Well," said Martha, "That's about twice as long a flight as the ones you're making in your exhibitions, which I must say are doing really well for A&E business. How would we get the flyer to Aurora?"

"Well," said Frank, "One way would be to fly her to Aurora from the fairgrounds. If some bigwig went along, then we'd get more news stories. Another way, since we'll be coming to Springfield from Tulsa on the Frisco, and the tracks go through Aurora, we could off-load the flyer on the way in."

"What's the country like between Aurora and Springfield?" asked Fred.

"Generally, it's woody and hilly," Frank answered. Not so good if you had to come down. At the cost of a bit longer time in the air, you could fly close to the roads. The airplane would still beat a truck on the route, because the plane doesn't stop for crossroads or slow for traffic, and it'd 'straighten out' the road's curves – wouldn't have to follow 'em in detail.

"I really do think it'd be best to bring the flyer to the fairgrounds and fly her to Aurora. That gives us the publicity we'd get from taking a bigwig on the trip, and we'd avoid holding up the train while unloading the flyer at Aurora."

"Well," Martha said, "Let's see what we might be able to set up. Ask Mr. Jennings of the Fair Committee what he thinks, and if he's interested in our doing it, see who he thinks might want to be flown to Aurora. He hesitated over our fee for the flyer. Maybe this'd sweeten him up.

"And check with the printer – how many catalogs will there be, how big a bundle, what'll they weigh?"

"Already checked the catalogs, Mother," said Frank. "Three hundred catalogs, filling one mail sack, total weight 45 pounds. Printer will run off another three hundred for use in case of accident, for $28.50."

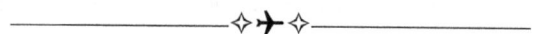

Tuesday, July 1, 1913, was a splendid day in Southwestern Missouri. Scattered clouds about a thousand feet above the ground drifted in a light, steady southwesterly breeze.

The previous morning, Aurora Alderman James Wilson, over the tearful objections of Ava, his wife, was flown from the Greene County fairgrounds to the field behind Aurora's new high school, where the Aurora Hound-dogs football team practiced, and from which the A & E flyer would depart with catalogs for the Fair's stock sale.

Ava hadn't been on hand to greet James when he arrived safely. Her son's pride and joy, a 1910 Ford Model T, had been delayed twenty minutes by a flat tire suffered just outside Billings. But both the Springfield Republican and the St. Louis Post Dispatch had taken care to have photographers on hand at both ends of the route, and their pictures in the two cities' papers had done all the Fair and circus managements could have wished.

As he had done on Monday, Frank scheduled Tuesday's flight for 9 am, before July heat had time to generate bumpy air. Alderman Wilson had a smooth trip.

Springfield's fairgrounds had been closed for Monday's departure, so there wasn't much of a crowd to see the takeoff. Just A&E mechanic Bob Petty, watching nervously over the flyer, the two newspaper photographers, pilot Frank Ellis, James and Ava Wilson, and Tom Jennings from the Fair Committee.

But there was no closing of Aurora High's practice field on Tuesday, and a considerable crowd had gathered to see the new miracle. "Mr. Forester," Frank said to Aurora's one policeman, "We've got to get folks away from the takeoff path. If we don't, unless we cancel, there'll be bloodshed when a propeller hits someone. Of course, we will have to cancel."

Guy Forester hastily deputized four stalwart men for crowd control. They had only limited success in clearing a path for the flyer's takeoff.

Bob Petty had the sack of stock-sale catalogs tied carefully in the flyer's passenger seat, and when the mob seemed fairly clear, Frank motioned to him to start the flyer's engine. Bob pulled down hard on the starboard propeller. When the Wright four-cylinder crackled into noisy life, the crowd melted away in panic. If anyone was going to catch a propeller, the flyer would have to chase him!

Guiding the flyer into the air, Frank climbed about a hundred feet above the ground and turned north-west. The Frisco tracks guided him to Missouri Highway 60, paved in asphalt through Aurora but graveled with clay soil outside town.

Helped by the south-easterly wind, the flyer's twin propellers pushed her steadily along – Marionville, Billings, and just after they left Republic, Frank could see the outskirts of Springfield. He kept on the northwesterly course until he saw the tall circle of Audrey and Ellis's Ferris wheel on the fairground.

That landmark got him to the field beside the fairground from which the flyer would operate. It was fifteen minutes until ten, and a sizeable mob had collected to see the "A & E Air Freight" arrive.

Frank dropped the Flyer down to about fifty feet above the ground and flew over the field on the north-west course. The wind sock that Bob had set up in the northwest corner of the field showed that he'd want to land going southeast. He flew clear of the field and turned to fly into the wind, back the way they'd come.

Setting the flyer into an easy dive, he aimed at a spot about twenty yards into the field. As the flyer crossed into the air over the field, Frank rounded gently out of the dive to fly a foot or so over the grass. Just before they reached the landing spot he'd picked out, Frank pulled the cord that stopped the flyer's engine. Pulling gently on the left control rod, he held her up until she lost speed and dropped firmly onto the grass.

"Your catalogs, Mr. Jennings!" said Frank as a grinning Tom Jennings came up to the flyer, with the Republican and Post-Dispatch photographers not far behind. Strangely, the mailbag with the catalogs began to move, and a skinny twelve-year-old boy wriggled out from under the sack.

Tom grabbed the miscreant and held him firmly. Tom and Frank, and the boy looked at one another. And broke simultaneously into uncontrollable laughter!

When at length the laughter stopped, Frank said to the boy, "Never do it again, Son. I mean that. Now, since you're experienced with airplanes, would you like a job? Bob Petty and I need somebody to help keep the flyer and her hanger clean, and to run errands while we're in Springfield."

The boy looked at Frank with an expression close to worship. "Yes, Sir," he said.

Chapter 10
QUESTIONS AND ANSWERS

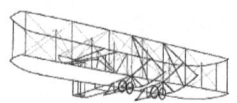

A golden October afternoon gave A&E perfect weather for their next-to-last stand of 1914, in Minden, Louisiana. Jill's horses dashed through their routines with zest, the clowns' staged pleasure in their acts looked real, and even ponderous Tusker and Shannah seemed to move lightly.

Frank Ellis brought the crowd to their feet as he put the A&E flyer through her paces, to which he'd added an item. Having practiced entering and recovering from a spin until he was confident with the maneuver, he ended his act by starting a spin from eight hundred feet up, about fifty feet in front of the crowd, then recovering out of the spin into a dive and rounding out flying level, headed straight at the center of the crowd. Turning away from the crowd, he exited, rocking the flyer's wings, waving goodbye.

Jill Coffee always watched Frank's act. Martha Ellis never did.

Frank and Bob Petty had just finished tucking the flyer into her tent when a young man walked up to them. "Wow," he said, "Walt ought to see that act!"

Astonished, Frank turned to face the stranger, then started a handshake that turned into an embrace, with much pounding of backs. "Where have you sprung from, Dave Galet? And why didn't you let me know you were coming?"

"Well," said Dave, "You're down here in my country. I live in New Orleans, you know. We use our flyer to advertise our cotton business. Well, we say that, but really it's just a way for me to keep my hand in and use my FAI ticket. I came up to Minden when I learned Audrey and Ellis were comin' to town. There's something I want to tell you. What are you doin' for dinner tonight?"

Frank answered, "Well, remember I'm a workin' man. But I just might be able to rustle up some feminine company, if you could hold on till around nine or ten."

So Frank Ellis and Dave Galet dined in Shreveport around midnight, with Jill Coffee and another rider, Mae Jennings. After leaving the women at Jill's quarters in the A&E train, Frank and Dave went for a companionable nightcap.

"And what is this you want to tell me?" asked Frank.

"Well," said Dave, "There's a chance to get in some real interesting flying in the war. There's an American flying squadron organizing, the Escadrille Américaine, for American volunteers to fly for France. They'd take you in a flash, Frank, they sure wouldn't have to teach you to fly, and you've got the FAI ticket. I'm going to give it a go. The French consul in New Orleans is my contact.

"Dave, that's interesting, all right, but A&E just has one pilot. I couldn't leave the show without a replacement, and there isn't one. I've tried to talk Bob Petty into taking the Wright course, but he's got the itch for higher education – saves his money for an electrical engineering degree at U of A."

"Well, Frank, let me know if you change your mind. I'll head out for France sometime around next April. Here's my card - my address and telephone numbers are on the back.

Dave and Mae's first child, Frank Galet, flew P-40s in World War II. Mae told Jill that she always worried when Dave was flying, but that was nothing compared to her heart-wrenching anxiety when her son Frank started pilot training.

Raindrops and occasional hail from an early November storm spattered the windows of the Ellis ranch house. A good fire warmed the largest room, decorated with pictures and trophies of the Audrey–Ellis Circus. The room's snug comfort couldn't warm the cold fact that the family was getting together to decide if the Audrey and Ellis Circus would show in the 1915 season.

"Well, Martha, it's your show, said Fred Ellis. "The airplane gives us a bump in crowds, but it doesn't do much more than manage the debts for the machine and the new seats.

"Joe Moore at the bank will give us the usual loan to get started, and Jill and the other bottom-of-the-bill[2] folks have said they'll go with us."

"There's a point to consider about the airplane," said Frank. "I hate to say it, but the truth is, she really isn't the best airplane today. Glen Curtiss, up in Hammondsport, New York, turns out better planes. They're a lot more powerful than our flyer. It's tough to say, but though our plane has a lot more flying in her, and I expect folks will still come to see what the two of us can do, she's going to make A&E look dated. In publicity stunts, we can beat a Lizzie if somebody wants to race, and a train's no match for us unless it's got

---

[2] Shows' advertisements described their star acts last.

a long straightaway, but we'd lose to a Curtiss plane and pilot unless we could beat 'em on turns. And Curtis pilots are darn good."

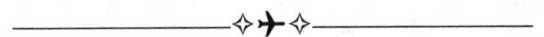

Auction Sale

On Friday, December 4 and Saturday at December 5, 1914 starting at 1 pm at the Ellis Ranch, Route 1, Purdy, Arkansas, Brown and Fedder Auctioneers will sell at auction certain property of the Audrey and Ellis Circus, including tents, railroad flat cars and Pullman cars, seating, electric generators, lighting, and a Wright Model B Flyer aeroplane. Terms are 10 per cent cash or certified check, with the balance due December 30, 1914, at the Brown and Fedder office, 23 Second Street, Fort Smith, Arkansas. The property will be available for inspection at the Ellis Ranch, December 2 and December 3, from noon until 5 pm.

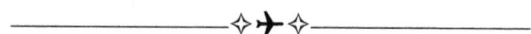

"It's just what Kipling says," said Jill Coffee, handing Frank Ellis an after-dinner balloon of good brandy. "Four things greater than all things are – 'Women and horses and power and war.' I'm glad that at least he put us first."

"Oh, come on, Jill. You'd put horses first." Frank Ellis found Jill as attractive and as contrary as anyone he knew. He had responded to her invitation to a joint farewell dinner for the two of them. Jill's widowed mother and Frank's parents, free from the Audrey–Ellis Circus, were traveling together for the March sun in Key West.

In two days, Jill would leave Purdy, with horses, to join the Ringling Brothers – Barnum and Bailey Circus in Sarasota, Florida. Tomorrow, Frank would leave for New Orleans to join Dave Galet on a voyage to Bordeaux, whence they'd travel to Paris and volunteer for service in the French Armée de l'Air, Quadrille Americaine.

"Is your mother enjoying the trip?" Frank asked, making conversation.

"Yes, I suppose so," Jill answered. "I've had one letter."

"Well," said Frank, she's a better correspondent than my folks. They sent a postcard the day after they got to Key West."

"Oh, nuts," Frank burst out, standing. He held out both hands. "You don't need me to tell you again how I feel about you."

Jill sat still. She felt that he must hear the beating of her heart. She who was always so controlled, so decisive, stood, uncertain. Frank took her in his arms, whose trembling belied their strength. They kissed. And kissed, again and again. Arms and hands clutched and caressed. No longer uncertain, Jill led him to her bedroom.

They stripped away interfering clothing. Naked, they beheld one another, then in an ecstasy of glad giving and hungry taking, they fell together onto the bed. Later, passion at last spent, they slept.

The child they made that night would never know his father. To the end of her days, Jill said only that he was brave and strong and young, lost in the Great War.

PART THREE

Chapter 11

TO FRANCE

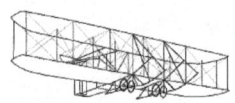

The opulence of the Galet residence in New Orleans fairly took Frank Ellis' breath away. "Gosh, Dave," he muttered, "The cotton business must be doin' all right!"

"Well," said Dave Smith, leading Frank to a guest room. "A showplace is part of the cotton business. A successful broker has to look the part. But, yeah, the war does make good times for sellin' cotton. It'll help us get to France, too. Plenty of boats are going. We'll be off on the Minérve tomorrow, takin' bales of the money-makin' stuff to Bordeaux. You'll see – the 'ol Minérve is sort of in the Galet family."

"Do we have to dodge torpedoes on the way?" Frank asked.

"Well, we're goin' on an American-flagged vessel," said Dave. "Mr. Wilson's neutrality ought to keep the subs off us. But, of course, the two of us are an example of the US 'neutrality.' Are you a pretty good swimmer?"

"Not much experience in salt water," Frank observed.

"Not to worry," said Dave. "A freighter full of cotton takes a long time to sink – the bales need a while to soak."

"Ah," said Frank.

Next morning, after a grand breakfast of beignets and chicory coffee, Frank and Dave were driven to the Port of New Orleans and boarded the Minérve, Captain André DuBois. "Bonjour, Oncle," said Dave, shaking the captain's hand.

"Bonjour, Neveu," replied the captain. "Parisians smile at our language," Dave told Frank, "But we snicker at theirs, too. *So* prissy. And we communicate well enough."

"And some of us manage to get along in a kind of English, too," said the captain, smiling.

The Minérve actually belonged to the Galet Frères firm, always available to change routes at the business's convenience. Quite in keeping with New Orleans traditions, she set a good table. Balancing that, Frank and Dave made regular runs on deck as she plowed along eastward. Oncle André usually went along, setting a pace that kept the younger men puffing.

The first warship sighted was, thankfully, not German but French: a trim destroyer sped briskly past the Minérve as she entered the approach to Bordeaux.

Two weeks and two days after leaving New Orleans, the Minérve docked at the Port of Bordeaux. The next day, Dave and Frank were on a train for la Gare du Midi in Paris. If Dave's Cajun got smiles from the Bordelais and Parisians, they understood it well enough.

Taxi from the station to the Hotel du Palais got Frank and Dave a night's rest. In the morning, bearing their pilot logbooks, FAI licenses and much other documentation, they began the circuitous process of volunteering for service in L'Esquadrille Americaine. (Later, after Germany complained officially about neutral

Americans fighting for the Kaiser's enemies, the squadron was renamed "Esquadrille LaFayette.")

They descended from the Metro at Fort de Nogent and walked to the Paris recruiting station of the Foreign Legion. They were expected, thanks to the French consul in New Orleans, M. Emile Boulay. A quick but thorough review of their documents, verifying that everything agreed with M. Boulay's correspondence, and an officer of the French Foreign Legion addressed them.

"Messieurs, je vous souhaites bienvenu au nom de la France. I welcome you in the name of France."

At this point, Frank and Dave broke away from the normal entry to the French Foreign Legion. Other volunteers would complete enlistment in Aubagne, but because they were already experienced pilots, as testified by their AFI licenses and logbooks, after passing medical and physical exams they were issued "brevets" certifying them as "pilotes d'avion," and also clothing and railway transport passes for Pau, where they'd complete their "formation" as pilots in an "école de perfectionnement." Then, they'd transfer from the Legion to the "Armée de l'Air" as non-commissioned officers, and report for duty with "L'Escadrille Americaine."

This circuitous route to service in the American Squadron kept the pair from swearing loyalty to France, which, as American citizens, they were not allowed to do.

Frank wrote letters to Walt Brookins about his training as a French pilot. Eventually, they reached him.

Chapter 12
PREPARING FOR COMBAT

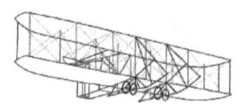

Dear Walt,

Dave Galet and I think you might care to hear about our experiences flying for the French. Here goes. The letters have to pass the censors, but I understand that they pass undated training information, while cutting out anything to do with actual operations.

Technically, Dave and I are volunteers for the French Foreign Legion. Our AFI licenses and our log books were deemed sufficient to justify the French aeronautical rating, the "brevet" or license, of "Pilote d'Avion" when we volunteered. That brevet signifies a flier who is prepared for the second step in training for French combat pilots, the "Ecole de Perfectionnement." Accordingly, we were assigned to an EP at a base near Pau.

Located north of the city, the base is at Pau in no small part because Wilbur Wright established the Wrights' flying activities there in 1909. When Dave and I arrived, several courses were active at Pau, including beginning pilot training and the EP.

The EP course didn't rely over much on students' experience, and I was damn glad of it. Modern combat airplanes are much lighter and much more powerful and consequently much faster and more maneuverable than the Wright Flyer, and I knew I would need all the help I could get.

The course was exactly what I needed. Dave and I were apprehensive about changing from the Flyer's hand controls for pitch, roll, and yaw, to hand control on a single stick for pitch and roll, with yaw control by feet. We needn't have worried. Both of us found that the new controls became quite natural almost immediately,

At the EP, we flew three or four short flights daily, weather permitting, largely on Nieuport 10 biplane machines, sometimes on Farmans, sometimes on Morane-Saulnier parasol-winged monoplanes. The last is a devil with an evil mind, always ready to fall off on a wing and kill the unwary pilot.

The MS responds very quickly to small control inputs, almost just suggestions. Perhaps this rapid maneuverability gives some advantages in combat, but I was deeply grateful to be done with it, and I hoped never to have to fly one again.

No longer the best French planes for combat, the Farman, the N10 and MS machines certainly permitted me to move from the Flier to the Nieuport 11s without killing myself, and I will always have grateful regards for the N10.

In addition to flying, the course included lectures on recognizing German aircraft – and, to be sure, also on recognizing Allied machines. It does not do to down one of our own!

Other lectures covered bomb dropping (it is no simple task to know where a bomb loosed from a fast-moving airplane and falling through turbulent air will land), and, particularly, trajectories of artillery fire. Artillery shells have a troublesome habit of climbing into altitudes occupied by aircraft, and pilots must know, from seeing artillery on the ground and knowing their shells' trajectories to likely targets, what segments of the sky are well avoided.

We also practiced "réglage," airborne assistance to artillery. For this work, airplanes have an observer as well as a pilot. The pilot flies over a target for artillery. The observer radios the arrival to the officer in charge of the guns, who fires one shot to begin the engagement. The observer notes the location of the shell-burst from that shot, and radios back "far" or "near," and "left" or "right" or "on target." With this information, the gun is adjusted and fired again.

This process continues iteratively until the shell bursts on the target, whereupon barrage after barrage is fired, pointed with the directions developed by réglage. It is a wearing procedure, but it pretty well guarantees the target's eventual destruction.

When Dave and I completed the Ecole de Perfectionnement, we became eligible for assignment to real war work. Since we were to serve in a combat unit, however, we were allowed to progress to the Ecole de Combat to receive training in air combat. I'll write about the EC later.

Best regards,

Frank

Dear Walt,

Dave's and my Ecole de Combat training continued at Pau. At first, the work seemed a significant step backward. We, who had been flying daily, were assigned to develop our skills in taxiing. This made sense, however, because the machines we'd fly in combat are lighter than those we'd been flying in the Ecole de Perfectionnement, and are consequently harder to control on the ground.

Beginning students at the EC start by mastering taxiing a Blériot monoplane with shortened wings, like a chicken with feathers trimmed so it can't fly.

This "Penguin" is the very dickens to control. It'll roll over at the slightest opportunity. You have to keep its tail flying at just the right angle, or it'll either nose over or fail to answer the rudder. To pass the course, you've got to make it do six straight lines on the ground, and I'm ashamed to tell you how many days – <u>days</u>, mind you – it took me to meet this "modest" requirement. Dave did it one day faster.

Having at last conquered the Penguin, the student practices taking off and landing a 30 hp Bleriot monoplane. That's about the same power as the Flyer, of course, but the Bleriot is "nervous cattle." Climbs fast and is very touchy on the controls. This flying is simple – all straight lines.

The next step is to the 50 hp Bleriot, and at last the student does real flying. Like the 30 hp machine, this Bleriot is touchy. It is demanding of the pilot, particularly because it doesn't glide worth a cuss. You pretty well need to dive to get it on the ground. The 50 hp work continues, with figure eights and landings on a prescribed spot.

Then, for my sins, came the very difficult Morane-Saulnier Parasol. As I said, it is a demon. If you can handle it, you can handle anything. I survived and passed this part of the course. With regularity that is becoming monotonous, Dave finished first.

The next step in the combat course doesn't employ airplanes. Instead, the students go to the machine gun school at Casso. I'll tell you about that in my next.

Frank

Dear Walt,

Dave and I traveled to the mitrailleuse (machine gun) course in the southwest of France. Each division of the French armed forces has its own separate school here.

The machine-gun school for the Armée de l'Air deals with the challenging task of hitting a moving target with a moving gun. The student first shoots from the rear cockpit of a two-man airplane, trying to hit a stationary balloon. This seems to call on eye-brain functions different from those used to hit a target, either stationary or moving, while standing on solid earth. Anyway, the skill takes some time to acquire. With what is becoming monotonous regularity, Dave was scoring regular hits several days before I could manage it.

But, manage it I did, and we both moved on to the still more challenging task of hitting a moving target from an airplane in flight. The targets were now towed on barges, floating in a lake.

Again, it took several days to develop reasonable results, but develop them, Dave and I did. You don't need me to tell you who got them first.

Armed with new skills, Dave and I returned to Pau to gain skill in stunts useful, nay, vital, for winning air combats.

And here, for the one and only time, I progressed a little faster than Dave. This was no credit to my aptitude; flying for the circus, I was mostly performing stunt after stunt, while Dave was making long straight trips for the cotton business.

The first stunt to master is the loop. It's not too hard to do, but it always impressed the circus crowds. One begins by lowering the nose to gain speed, then hugging the stick to get a steep climb. Eventually, the plane stalls and falls over backward into a dive.

Recovery from the dive is then straightforward; one releases the stick and, once a normal dive is achieved, recovers from it in the usual way.

Other simple stunts, like side-slips, in which the pilot "crosses" the controls, pushing the stick one way, and applying rudder in the opposite direction. The airplane then "slips" in the direction opposite to the one commanded by the stick.

By no means simple is the "vrille," or spin. The spin is a stable mode of flight, in which the machine "spins" about a vertical axis while pointing straight down. A well-designed airplane doesn't "want" to spin, so the pilot must force it to abandon its basic instincts. He does this by lifting the nose while cutting off power. When the plane stalls, the pilot presses hard on the rudder for one side or the other.

The machine then begins the spin, headed straight down and spinning about the vertical. The view outside the cockpit is, frankly, terrifying. One is hurtling rapidly down and spinning. Without prompt and effective piloting, a crash follows.

To leave the spin, the pilot applies the rudder opposite to the spin to stop it. The airplane is now heading straight down, not yet under control. To gain control, the pilot moves the stick slowly forward until the plane enters a dive, from which recovery is straightforward.

The plane loses 2 or 3 hundred feet with each turn of the spin, so one must begin recovery in a timely way. The maneuver is helpful for evading an attack, as Dave and I were to find out in service.

In the final part of L'Ecole de Combat, student pilots engage in mock battles, one-on-one, or in coordinated attacks by groups, "flights," of planes.

In single combat, one tries to attack from a direction in which his opponent's gun cannot bear. For a single-pilot machine, this is, of course, from the rear.

Should one find an enemy behind him, he must change that state of affairs promptly. If your machine can climb faster than the enemy's, a loop may put you on his tail, with fatal results for him. If his plane can both climb and turn faster than yours – a most unpleasant situation – a spin may enable you to break off the engagement. There have been cases in which the pursued pilot lured his enemy into a low altitude from which he found himself unable to recover before striking an obstacle on the ground.

At last, Dave and I graduated from the combat school and set out for service with the American Squadron. This must be the last of these letters, because any discussion of operations is strictly forbidden. After the war, you and Dave and I can get together and yak away to our hearts' content.

Frank

Chapter 13

WAR, LOVE, AND DEATH

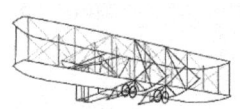

Well, after all that training, real action at last. Captain Thénault wisely sends new additions on their first patrol out with old hands, and I'm lucky to go with Kiffin, Charlie and Mike.

O.k., Kiffin is up, so full throttle, build speed, forward stick to get the tail flying, build speed, gently back on the stick, and we're off. This Nieuport 11 is a saucy little thing. Climbs like it's eager to fight.

Into formation, Kiffin on my left, Charlie and Mike behind us. Keep climbing, keep a sharp lookout.

Six thousand feet. Level off, keep formation on Kiffin, scan below and to the right. It's my job to spot Boche in the air.

Over enemy territory now. Really concentrate on the search.

Time to turn for home, with enough gas for an engagement if we spot Boche.

Still no Boche. Concentrate, Frank! Don't miss an enemy.

Getting close to the end of our range. Still no enemy.

Kiffin wags his wings, points down and ahead! There they are!

Four Fokkers, clearly headed for home. We've got just enough gas for a try at them.

The one on their left is for me. Tight right turn, dive, keep the Fokker in sight. Try to get below him.

O.k., now, just below his altitude. Work in to get below and behind him, close in.

He's seen me! Too far to shoot; let's see what he does. He climbs! Well, the Bébé can beat his Fokker at that game. Up we go. Boy, he's climbing like blazes. So are we. Are we closing? A little, anyway. Christ, he's pulling into a loop. Is he trying to get behind me and turn the tables on me? No! He just wants to gain some separation.

He snaps into a turn. Oho, he's scooting for home on his original course.

Have I got enough gas to chase him? No, and Kiffin and Charlie are nowhere in sight. They've made the decision for me. I settle in for the trip home, always looking for Boche. Perhaps I'll have better luck another day.

I land, following Kiffin and Mike. Taxi to the line. Stop, cut the gas. The engine stops. I'm drained. There's sweat inside my suit.

As I step off Bébé's wing onto the grass, Kiffin walks up. "Not bad, Frank. You had him on the run. A little more gas and you could've got him."

I grin. "Thanks, Kiffin." Tomorrow morning we'll go out on patrol again.

Northwest Arkansas Record, July 13, 1916

Mr. and Mrs. Fred Ellis of Purdy were distressed to learn that their son, Frank Ellis, a pilot with the Lafayette Squadron in France, had been wounded in combat. The senior Ellises are assured that the young man is receiving excellent medical care, and his full recovery is confidently expected.

God damn the Boche. I'd only have a scratch if they weren't using explosive bullets. Thank God for French doctors. They assured me the leg would be good as new – "parfait" – in a few weeks, and it looks like they're right. Walking sure does help. Ouch! Don't twist it, Frank!

In the third week of his recovery, Frank was encouraged to walk. His walks took him through the pleasant country of northeastern France. A woman whose young face was marred by deep grief began appearing where a path crossed his road. At the third encounter, she spoke.

"Vous êtes blessé, m'sieu?" Frank had picked up just enough French from Dave's Creole and his weeks in France to reply.

"Oui, mam'selle. Mais ça n'est pas grave. C'est un tout p'tite rien."

"Mais, ma foi, vous parlez Français!

"Well, not really. I have a friend – j'ai un ami - from New Orleans. Nous sommes des pilotes d'avion.

"And me, I have une cousine in Saint Louis! Is close, Saint Louis, to La Novelle Orléans?

Thus they began. She learned he was Frank, from "l'Arkansas," and he learned that her two brothers, and "mon homme", whom she would now never marry, had perished in "cette guerre maudite." When she told him of her losses, she had the face of a bitter old woman.

Her name was Marie. For her, he was Francis. She invited him to her home, quite close along the path. Daily, his Creole became more French, less foreign.

He knew only too well how unlikely he was ever to see Jill again, and what was bound to happen, happened. In their lovemaking, Marie clutched him to her passionately, claiming payment of a debt.

A few days after Francis told her he was well enough to fly again, a lone Nieuport 17 flew low over Marie's home, circled it once, and flew away. She was glad to have had his visit. She knew that neither she nor "l'Arkansas" would ever see him again.

When in 1919 influenza made their child an orphan, an American–French organization, the Fatherless French Children's Society, rescued her.

Damn, Frank, what a stupid, clumsy thing to do! Bang your leg climbing into a plane! Gosh, it hurts! Well, give it a minute. That's better. O. k., taxi out. Line up, let Fred get away, full throttle, let her pick up speed, tail up, more speed, ease back on the stick, and away we go.

Calm day so far. No Boche. Leg still hurts. Must've really whacked it. Is that blood? Hell, the docs will ground me again!

Oho, spoke too soon about Boche! Golly, they're just pouring in from the east! Well, we can do something about that. Up and at 'em!

Hah! He was so busy getting away from me, he didn't see Fred! Oh, well done, Fred!

Damn, two of 'em on me! We're high enough – let's see if they've got the balls to chase me in a spin! Whoops, down we go!

By God, that one has got balls! O.k., Boche, you man enough to stay with me all the way?

Guess not! Away he goes, chicken! Now, quick, hard left rudder Christ, leg doesn't move!

Oh, God

Northwest Arkansas Record, October 23, 1916

Frank Ellis, son of Mr. and Mrs. Fred Ellis of Purdy, died in France on October 1 while flying in the Lafayette Squadron. Frank was well known and well liked throughout the southern United States as the pilot who gave remarkable exhibition flights with the old Audrey–Ellis Circus. Frank Ellis' military funeral was conducted in France, and by his wish, he is interred there, with his comrades who also perished in the war. Mr. and Mrs. Ellis will greatly appreciate condolences mailed to them at Rural Route 1, Purdy, Arkansas.

PART FOUR

Chapter 14

THE SEARCH BEGINS

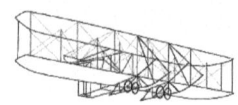

I never thought much about having an odd birthday. Born February 29, 1916, I always celebrated the first of March on non-leap years, just the way my folks started off. A Gilbert and Sullivan opera turns on the tangles such a birthday can cause, but I never had any.

Sometimes it does come up, though. Like this year, when I'm forced to retire at "Age 52." The FAA had no problem at all. For them, I turned 52 on March 1, 1968, and no fuss about it.

Janey in personnel had to laugh at me, though. "Gee, Mister Galet, you've only had 13 birthdays. You can't retire yet!" She's a sweet kid.

The shop gave me a nice sendoff. Mr. Jennings from headquarters said kind things about a career "pushing tin" from 1937 until 1968.

I did get to see the profession mature. The "tin" grew from DC-3's cruising at 130 knots to 707's tearing through the sectors at 480.

Well, I'm going to change from controlling flights to flying them. My Cessna 150 and I are setting out on a quest – we're going to look for an airplane.

It's a sort of family mystery. The plane is – probably was, I thought - a Wright B Flyer, made in 1912, about three years before me. And it belonged to a circus, which belonged to my family.

I say "family," but I'm friendship kin, not blood kin, to the folks who actually owned the circus. My dad and Frank Ellis, whose mother owned the show, flew together in the Lafayette Squadron in World War 1. Frank was the circus's pilot, flying exhibits in their Wright Flyer. I'm named for him. Dad got home from France, but Frank didn't.

Dad taught me to fly, although I had enough lessons from a certificated instructor to get my license when I was seventeen. I signed on with the old CAA after graduating from LSU, and, after I finished training in Oklahoma City, stayed with controlling, except for four years away flying P-40s in North Africa. The CAA obligingly let me have my job, with seniority, when I got back in 1945.

I've got my locker all cleaned out, and the stuff in a duffel bag. I'll swing by Cathy's and my place to pick up George, and then head for the airport – HFY, Indy South, Greenwood -- to start on the first leg of our travels. George is my bulldog. He's right at home in the Cessna. Cathy is my sister.

When Cathy was widowed, and Liz and I finally ended our rocky marriage, Cathy and I set up housekeeping in my place, west of Indianapolis. It was handy for my job.

George and Cathy, and I make a good group. I think Cathy's more partial to George than to me, but she puts up with her brother.

We're both adopted, me from the nuns at St. Edward's in Fort Smith, Cathy, circuitously, via the Fatherless French Children Society. FFCS did not facilitate the relocation of French orphans. It arranged for Americans to provide financial support for fatherless French children. Somehow, the Galets' relation with Cathy changed from support to adoption. I can imagine Grand-père Galet's money playing a role. I can just remember when Cathy arrived. I was three.

Chapter 15

THE BANDLEADER

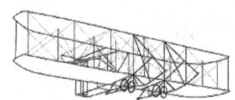

It was a pleasant hop from Indianapolis to Evansville, EVV. Parked the Cessna with the fixed-base operator, picked up a rental car, and got George and me checked into a Holiday Inn in good time for supper. After dinner, I called Paul Kieth at his assisted-living residence to be sure he was expecting me the next morning. He insisted that I join him for breakfast.

"Hello, Frank," said Paul, opening the door to his apartment. "Thanks for coming to see an old crock!"

He certainly didn't look like an old crock. Slender, Paul carried his eighty-odd years very well indeed.

"I thank you for seeing me, sir," I told him. We went to the facility's dining room for a pleasantly surprising breakfast – more home-like than institutional.

Over coffee, I beamed. "What a good place you have," I said.

"Well, it certainly suits me," said Paul Kieth. "Now tell me more about this 'airplane hunt' that brings you here."

"Well, sir, you know that when Audrey-Ellis sold up, their Wright Flyer was part of the auction. Those airplanes are of considerable interest nowadays, and the ones that have been kept – there aren't many – are pretty much treasured.

"I'm a brand-new retiree, unmarried, with time on my hands, an airplane to fly around in, and I'm really curious. Nobody seems to know what became of the A & E Flyer. I'm going to try to find out, just to satisfy my curiosity."

"A quest, eh?"

"Yes, sir, that's it. And I'll be glad to learn about the people at A & E – Frank Ellis, Bob Petty, Jill Coffee. I'm going to visit Bob and Jill."

"Well, let me see if I know anything helpful. Golly, thinking about A & E sure does bring back memories. Of course, everybody in the show knew Frank Ellis and Jill Coffee. Jill was so pretty and so charmingly friendly with everybody. She got to be bottom-of-the-bill – you know what that means?"

"Yes, sir, those were the stars of the show – their acts were featured last on flyers and posters."

"That's right. Well, she put together a terrific act with horses from her folks' ranch, and the stunts she pulled off were the equal of anything in the big shows. She started with A&E when she was just sixteen, and I know Ringling and Mighty Haag both got after her right quick. She stayed loyal to A & E, and Fred and Martha Ellis sort of came to think of her as part of their family.

"Frank Ellis certainly didn't have any brotherly affection for Jill Coffee, though. Altogether a different kind!

Of course, Frank and Jill knew one another all the time they were growing up. Frank was, oh, three years older than Jill, and the

Ellis and Coffee ranches were 'neighbors' - about two miles between ranch houses.

"Fred Ellis was grooming Frank to manage A & E. He and Martha scrupulously kept him in school through high school – roomed him with the Ellis ranch manager and his wife while they toured with A & E, until school let out every year – and they worked hard to keep the show going. That wasn't easy, particularly in the first couple of years after Bill Eagan died and willed it to Martha.

Frank got a real thorough introduction to circus life. He was into everything on the lot, except the band. I'd've been glad to have him, but he didn't have much interest in any instrument.

"He never was a big kid, sort of "well-knit," I guess you'd say, but when he got his growth spurt at about seventeen, he muscled up pretty well, and he even learned to sling a mallet with the tent gang putting up the big top. His grandad, Bill Eagan, had him in the office most of one whole season, so he knew how the dollars came in and went out. Frankly, as with all the shows, balancing those two for A&E was quite an act.

"Frank was always into any kind of machinery. When Fred began agitating for electric lights, around 1908, Frank was red hot for the idea. Martha was careful and insisted that they put in electric lights just for the dressing tents and office, and to light the paths where customers came in and got into the stands, to see how it worked.

"Well, it worked o.k., and it sure was safer than the torches it replaced. So, in 1910, they got a big Westinghouse generator and lots of wiring, and lit up A & E. Worked quite well, except the big generator was hard to start sometimes. Frank always got it going, though, occasionally in the nick of time."

"Bob Petty was a runaway. Really, he ran off to the circus! I don't know if Bob ever found out, but his dad showed up at A&E one day, looking for Bob. Had a good long talk with Fred Ellis. Made a deal with Fred to let him know if Bob ever got in trouble, and let Bob stay with A & E."

I sure wasn't going to have trouble getting Paul to talk about the old days in A & E! Problem might be to shut him up.

"How did A & E folks feel about the airplane?"

"Well, they were just as proud as could be. They thought A&E was really leading the way. 'Take that, Ringling!' you might say.

"Jill Coffee got right into the spirit of the thing. It was her idea to work the airplane into the spec – you know what that is?"

"Yes – a spectacle right at the beginning of the show. Sometimes there was an ending spec, too.

"I never saw A & E's spec, but I hear that it was really a sight to see. Indians attacking a pioneer cabin, and Frank Ellis swooping down on 'em with the Flyer until soldiers rode up to chase 'em away."

"That's right. It really was something, back in 1913. Got A & E publicity all over, with photos in Springfield and Fort Smith and St. Louis papers. The New Orleans Picayune once gave it a special section."

"So, with the A&E having that draw, how come it couldn't keep showing?"

"Oh, all the circuses had money trouble most of the time. They needed lots of people and lots of transport. Railroads weren't too happy to have 'em – took lots of trouble to get 'em on and off consists, and they didn't haul circuses cheaply. It costs the circuses a lot to feed all their stock, and all their folks, too.

"And the airplane was expensive. I remember Fred Ellis saying that it's added draw just about paid for the cost of the plane, and of the extra seating they needed for the larger crowds it drew.

"Of course, Frank Ellis was family, so the pilot wasn't as big an expense as it might have been. And Bob Petty, A&E's engineering boss, pretty well took on the plane's extra maintenance himself because he liked it a lot.

"Still, like most of the shows, A&E just scraped along. Martha and Fred weren't getting any younger – you know, Martha was in a wheelchair after she had polio the year after her dad died and left her the show – and I think they also kinda got worn out with A&E. They began to talk about selling up.

"Jill Coffee and the Elephants' Watkinson brothers and the other bottom-of-the-bill acts were willing to hang on, but, like I said, I think Martha and Fred just got tired."

"So A & E's last show was in the fall of 1914, and Martha and Fred sold up in December of 1914. Was the Flyer in the sale?"

"Yes, I remember it was in a barn on the Ellis ranch, with fabric ropes keeping folks off of it, so folks could look it over before the sale, like all the sale items. I don't remember seeing the auctioneer actually knock her down, but he must have, and the new owner must have got her away before the sale ended on Saturday afternoon.

"Bob Petty might know how that happened – he or somebody who knew how to knock the Flyer down and pack her up to travel must have got her ready to move. Of course, all packed up, she wasn't a problem to transport. She got moved all the time, with A & E!"

"Were Martha and Fred and Frank Ellis, and Jill Coffee at the sale?"

"I remember Fred and Frank were there. I can't recall seeing Jill or Martha."

"Well, of course, Fred and Martha and Frank Ellis are gone. I am going to visit Bob Petty. He lives in Pittsburgh, retired big gun with Westinghouse. And I'm going to make Jill's place in Purdy my last stop. Jill and my folks are real good friends, you know. She'd visit us in New Orleans, and I got to work on her horse farm every summer while I grew up. She's my Aunt Jill!"

Chapter 16

THE RUNAWAY MATURED

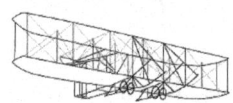

The next day was rainy, with a line of thunder-pumpers over the Indiana – Pennsylvania border, so I exercised the prudent pilot/old retired guy option of loafing around the Holiday Inn (nice pool, good-looking life guard, replaced too soon by a guy). Went for a long walk with George.

The next morning, we took off for Allegheny Airport, AGC, a general aviation airport serving Pittsburgh. It's just ten miles outside downtown. It's easy to rent a car there, and there are plenty of motels close by.

I'd never met Bob Petty. He was off to the U of A right away when A & E sold up, and he never came back to Purdy. I had been afraid that he might not be willing to give Frank Galet some time.

When we exchanged letters, he agreed to see me. And when I phoned up from my Best Western, he seemed really glad we were getting together.

Mr. Robert Petty's residence was a distinguished stone house on a hillside outside Pittsburgh. He opened his door when I rang, and looked me over for a moment.

"Mr. Galet, I presume?" he said with a smile.

"Yes, sir," I said, smiling back. "Thank you for seeing me!"

"My pleasure, I assure you," he replied, smiling back. "Westinghouse puts its VPs out to pasture when they turn 75, and I'm always ready to find something interesting to do. Your letter said you were Dave Galet's son, a pilot, retired controller, looking for A & E's Wright Flyer?"

"All correct, sir," I answered.

"Well," said Bob Petty (I couldn't for the life of me think of him as "Mr. Petty). "She was kinda my first big romance – long before I met Betty, of course."

"I'm glad to hear that last qualifier," said a grey-haired woman dryly, walking in to join us. "Mr. Galet, it's a pleasure. You cannot imagine how excited Bob has been since he got your letter. He never got that circus – or, particularly, that airplane, and the Frank Ellis who flew it – out of his blood. Come in, Frank, sit down, and have a cup of coffee."

Of course, I did that gladly. Turning to Bob Petty, I said, "I hear from Paul Kieth that the A&E Flyer was in their close-out auction. Did you see it there?"

"Sure," said Bob. "Frank Ellis and I helped the buyer's crew get her packed up, just like she was going off on an A & E move. The crew had two trucks. The auctioneer's clerk came in with some paperwork, a bill of sale and so on. The crew chief handed the clerk a check – I gathered he paid in full – the crew loaded the Flyer on their trucks, and off they went."

"Did anyone name the buyer?"

"Not that I heard. Frank and I were trying hard not to bawl – 'C'mon,' I remember Frank saying, 'It's just a piece of machinery."

"Yeah, I know," I said to Bob. "It's ridiculous to have affection for a machine. But you do. I sure did, for the P-40 I flew in North Africa."

Mrs. Petty looked at her husband and me. "And you find that ridiculous? Men are the strangest creatures," she said. "Where are you staying, Frank? Won't you spend a day or so with us? It would mean so much to Bob. He can tell you tales of the A&E Flyer until you get heartily sick of them."

Mrs. Petty graciously extended her invitation to George. He and the Pettys' Golden Retriever quickly made friends.

I had a wonderful time. Bob had a photo album, and I was glad to see Frank Ellis, his father and mother, and Aunt Jill as she looked in her riding days, and my mom back then. I didn't learn any more about the Flyer's whereabouts, but I certainly got a lot better acquainted with A & E. And with Bob Petty. We seemed to develop a surprisingly strong friendship across a generation, and I treasure it.

Bob told me about Frank's flying a load of stock catalogs twenty-five miles from the printer to the fairgrounds in Springfield, Missouri, in 1913, when that was still enough of a feat to get news coverage in Saint Louis and Springfield papers.

"A twelve-year-old kid stowed away under the catalogs," Bob said. "When he crawled out, I was ready to wallop him – talk about bad publicity, if there'd been a crash that killed him! – and I think Frank was, too. But then the whole thing struck Frank and me, and the kid, as irresistibly funny. We roared with laughter like lunatics. When sanity finally returned, Frank gave the kid a stern lecture, and – much to my surprise – offered him a job, helping keep the Flyer tidy and running errands. Kid worked his backside off all the time we were in Springfield. I've often wondered what became of him."

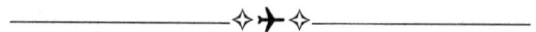

A novelist can answer such questions. The young man became an army pilot, flew C-47s over the hump in World War II, and, taking advantage of the GI Bill, became a veterinarian. His son took over his practice when he retired in 1971, and he died in 1985.

Chapter 17

THE DOG TRAINER

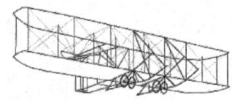

Otto Karsch had turned ninety and was living with his daughter, Gertrude, a veterinarian, in Springfield, Missouri. George and I made the trip from AGE to SGF with an overnight stop at home in Indianapolis.

My exchange of letters with Otto and Gertrude made it clear that they'd both be offended if I didn't stay with them. That was one stop where, after I assured Dr. Karsh that Fred was duly licensed in Indiana and that his shots were up-to-date, there was no trouble finding accommodations for George.

Dr. Karsch had invited me to lunch. "Dad never shows up much before lunch, nowadays," she explained.

I opened the door to Dr. Karsch's office a little before twelve. "Mr. Galet?" inquired the receptionist. "Dr. Karsch is with patients just now, but please make yourself comfortable, and she'll be with you a soon as she can. Is this George? We're expecting him." She and George vanished toward the kennel.

I believe Dr. Gertrude Karsch's home, office and kennel made up the happiest dwelling and workplace I ever saw. Two veterinary assistants, one male, one female, bustled about fetching and carrying patients to and from the boss's workspace. Barks were heard in the distance, but I thought, more friendly than ailing. Duly enrolled as a day boarder, George fit right in.

Dr. Karsch came to greet me a little after twelve. "Come on into the house," she said, leading the way. "Dad should join us pretty soon. He admits to ninety-three, and that's consistent with his naturalization papers, but I think he may be hiding a year or two.

"He loves being with my patients and boarders," Gertrude went on, "And I'm certain they and he are good for one another.

"He's looking forward to your visit. He seems to have enjoyed his time with – what was it, the Audley and Ellis show – about as much as anywhere he performed.

"Mother and I never toured with Dad," she went on. To be blunt, she and Dad didn't get along. But he had that good, strong Lutheran sense of responsibility, and he always supported us well.

"So you're trying to find an old Wright airplane?" she went on.

"Yes, Dr. Karsch. Those machines are important historical artifacts nowadays, and I'm retired with time on my hands and an airplane to travel about in, and I'm sort of in the Audrey–Ellis Circus family. My Dad and Frank Ellis flew together in World War I, and Jill Coffee, an A & E star, is such good friends with my folks that I grew up calling her Aunt Jill, and, finally, I'm a pilot – flew P40's in North Africa – anyway, as you say, I'm looking for the A & E Wright Flyer."

"I hope Dad can help," she said. By the way, please call me Gertrude, everybody does, and may I call you Frank?"

"I'll be honored," I responded. Just then, Otto Karsh joined us. I rose.

"Good afternoon, Mr. Karsh," I said, extending a hand. "Thank you for seeing me. I'm Frank Galet."

"You're for sure welcome," said the frail-looking nonagenarian, taking my hand. "Please sit." He sat as I did.

"But you're not Frank from the old A&E show, are you? He'd be much older!"

"No, sir, I'm not. Frank Ellis and my father, David Galet, flew together in World War I, and Mae Galet, my mother, who was Mae Jennings then, was one of the riders in Jill Coffee's equestrian show with A & E."

"And you're looking for the A & E airplane," said Otto Karsh.

"Yes, sir. I hope to find out what became of the plane, and I'm interested to hear about the people in the circus, too, people like Jill Coffee and Frank Ellis, Bob Petty and Paul Kieth, and so on.

"Heh, let me think. Well, I remember the people more than the airplane. Saw it in the show, of course. Frank Ellis flew it in the spec – you know spec?"

"Yes, sir, it was a performance in and over the ring, just at the end of the opening parade, and the Flyer was part of it when A & E showed outdoors."

"Right. And Frank would also fly a performance in those shows, too."

"Yes, Sir."

"Not so much of the 'Sir,' please. I'm Otto, and you're Frank."

"Thanks, Otto. I expect you remember a lot about the Audrey–Ellis circus."

"Sure! That was a good show! Fred Ellis saw to it that they always paid their people; some shady shows were said to 'red light' people when money got tight. You know what was 'red light'? "

"No, Otto. What was that?"

"Well, when a show got into tough times and money got short, bad managers would sometimes manage to leave some folks behind when the show pulled out. Let 'em stranded, broke. Maybe the manager would even sneak away alone with whatever money was left, and leave everybody behind. Criminal! But A & E was nothing like that. It was kinda Sunday School, too."

"I'm afraid I don't know 'Sunday School,' either," I confessed.

"Oh, some shows kept a high moral standard," said Otto. "Others maybe not so much. Girls maybe in the men's rooms. Men staggering about the lot drunk. But Martha Ellis never let any of that happen. Folks got fired! You could maybe have a quiet schnaps in your own place, but no carouse!"

"Did you know Frank Ellis or Jill Coffee, or Bob Petty?" I asked.

"Frank, sure, and Bob, sure. Jill was friendly to everybody, but she worked real hard at her act. Damn good act! Spent lots of time seeing to her horses. Awful pretty, though.

"Frank Ellis sort of grew up on the lot. Everybody knew Frank! I think his dad and granddad wanted him to take over the show someday.

"He was some older than Jill. He sure did take a shine to her! You could see it! But she was always working."

"Bob Petty ran away to the circus, you know. That happened, sometimes. In a good show like A&E, folks would look after a runaway, some, maybe even go together and buy him a ticket home. Bob Petty stayed with A & E, clear to the last show."

"Did you go to the sale when A & E closed down?"

"No, Frank. That must've been after the end of the 1914 season. Like always, after the circus went to quarters at Purdy, I always got my dogs on at an indoor show. Chicago, St. Louis, and one time in New Orleans! Had to make money – my girl wanted to be a vet, and that was gonna take some green!

"You kept on touring, Otto, for a good many more years. Did any of your shows ever have a Wright Flyer?"

"I don't think so, Frank. Airplanes changed a lot after the war, you know. Even I could tell they didn't look much like the A & E Flyer."

Gertrude went back to her practice after lunch, and Otto retired to nap. I was drafted to exercise some of the borders, and the afternoon passed pleasantly.

After supper, Gertrude Karsch went to look after two patients. When she returned, she looked at me half frowning, with a question.

"I know this is a strange thing to ask, but do you by any chance happen to play Parcheesi? It's a board game that dad and I play in the evenings."

I couldn't've been more pleasantly surprised. "Oh, do I! I thought Parcheesi was just the Galet family's secret vice! My folks and grandparents, and all their friends in New Orleans, are buggy about Parcheesi. They'd have disowned me if I didn't play!"

"Incredible!" Gertrude exclaimed. "I have to warn you, Dad is a demon player. But he's honest!"

Over hard-fought games, Gertrude talked about a Springfield pilot who volunteered his services and his airplane to rescue animals needing rapid transport. Interesting.

We got to bed pretty late. Otto the Parcheesi demon is a night hawk.

The next morning, I had to tug George away from his new friends at Gertrude's kennel. I hated to leave, too, but Aunt Jill was expecting the two of us.

Chapter 18

AUNT JILL

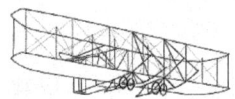

The Cessna took George and me from Springfield to the Coffee horse farm outside Purdy in just over two hours. Below us as we flew south-west, the gently rolling hills of the Ozark plateau sharpened and steepened, preparing for their plunge toward the Arkansas River. I'd flown into Aunt Jill's place before, and it was with a sense of homecoming that I saw familiar landmarks approaching her ranch.

The well-kept grass strip at the Coffee ranch was handy for Aunt Jill's customers, and I was glad to use it. Approaching from the north east, I flew over the field at twelve hundred feet above ground level. The wind sock indicated a moderate breeze out of the south west, and broadcasting my intentions on Unicom, I descended four hundred feet and circled to the right to enter a left downwind, turned on base leg a little downwind of the point where I planned to touch down, turned final, rounded out over the runway, cut the power, and held the Cessna off until her main wheels settled onto the grass.

Aunt Jill came out to greet George and me as I tied the Cessna down. She hugged me as I kissed her cheek, and scratched George's ears as he jumped up for attention.

The three of us walked to the house. Coming to Aunt Jill's place was coming home. George trotted off happily toward the barn, entranced by the symphony of scents rioting from all sides.

"Got burgers for lunch," Aunt Jill said, as we sat at her kitchen table. "And corn on the cob, fresh off the stalk." Sounded good to me. We munched and chomped away.

"How are your folks?" she asked. Did they come to Indiana for your Freedom Birthday?"

"Yes," I said. "Not so much 'freedom' as 'out to pasture.' But I'm having a good time, looking for the A&E Flyer. Visited Paul Kieth, Bob Petty, and Otto Karsch."

"My goodness," said Jill Coffee, "What a crew! How are they?"

"Paul is happy and loquacious. Bob and I have become fast friends, and his wife is adorable. Otto is failing a bit, but he plays a mean game of Parcheesi. His daughter's a vet; her patients and boarders satisfy his need for animal pals. Did you know Bob Petty was a runaway?

"Sure. There are precious few secrets in a traveling circus. I think I knew your folks were going to get married before your mom did. For sure, I knew it before your dad did."

"Us limited menfolk are always outmatched in the battle of the sexes," I observed. It was kind of Aunt Jill not to mention Liz.

"And, by the way, you were on hand when A & E sold up. What can you tell me about where their Flyer ended up?

"Oh, not much. I stayed away from the sale with Martha Ellis. She hated to give up the show. Thought her father wouldn't have forgiven her for letting it go. Poor lady, Fred Ellis and I tried to calm her down, but she cried."

Presently, Aunt Jill went to see to her charges - there were twenty-one of them that Saturday - and I went to stretch my legs.

The Coffee Ranch was a good place for a walk. Two rows of stables and a barn stretched out back of the house, beyond the house and barn of the overseer's home. Beyond that were two corrals, and on beyond them were meadows, and then woods of maple and oak stretched for the rest of the ranch's 80 acres. Purdy township is one of the loveliest parts of what was New France, until in 1803, President Jefferson bought it for three cents an acre when Napoleon Bonaparte found himself hard-pressed for francs. Growing up in New Orleans – La Nouvelle Orléans – I was frequently reminded of my French heritage by grandmére et grandpére. Cathy, who is more French than I am, finds the whole Creole business silly. But, of course, women are the practical sex.

George joined me as I returned to Aunt Jill's horse-training area. Suddenly, driven by goodness knows what, he dashed off into the barn.

Like all barns, this one was dim. It smelled of horses and hay. George barked furiously at the foot of a ladder that led up to the hayloft. What could be possessing him?

I climbed the ladder. Just as my head cleared the floor of the loft, a black cat launched itself over me, lit athletically on the barn floor, and tore out the door before George could shift himself into pursuit.

I'd been into the hayloft dozens of times while working for Aunt Jill, but something possessed me to go up into it and look around.

The loft covered both sides of the barn, with a twenty-foot gap in the middle. Idly, I strolled over the footbridge connecting the halves. Hay supplies were mostly on the other side, but a few bales and an ancient carriage were on this one.

I'd noticed the carriage when I worked for Aunt Jill, but it never seemed particularly interesting, and I never bothered with it. I walked up to the coach and peered inside.

Perished upholstery occupied both front and back ends of the conveyance. There was quite a bit of space beyond it. My eyes lit on a wooden crate in the space beyond. There were three crates. Two were narrow, about fifty feet long and five feet high. Beside them was a roughly cubical crate, about ten feet on a side. They looked as though they'd been in the barn a long time.

I knew, as surely as I knew I breathed, that my search for the A & E Flyer was over. I climbed down from the loft and went into the house for a talk with Aunt Jill. After that, I thought, George and I would go to Springfield.

www.ingramcontent.com/pod-product-compliance
Lightning Source LLC
Chambersburg PA
CBHW060043230426
43661CB00004B/637